The Princeton Review

Cracking

the Virginia SOL:

EOC Algebra I

by Kevin Higginbotham

Random House, Inc.
New York

www.randomhouse.com/princetonreview

The Independent Education Consultants Association recognizes The Princeton Review as a valuable resource for high school and college students applying to college and graduate school.

Princeton Review, L.L.C.
2315 Broadway
New York, NY 10024

E-mail: comments@review.com

Published in the United States by Random House, Inc., New York.

ISBN 0-375-75561-6

Editor: Russell Kahn
Designer: Evelin Sanchez-O'Hara

Manufactured in the United States of America

9 8 7 6 5 4 3 2 1

Dedication

To Avery Johnson

Acknowledgments

I'd like to acknowledge Russell Kahn, my editor, for his invaluable assisitance. Thanks also to Mary Ann Cromeek for her sharp eye.

Contents

Part I

About the Test

Chapter 1

Introduction

The End-of-Course Exams

The end of what? Well, it's not *the* end. The End-of-Course (EOC) exams are only the final exams for certain "core" courses offered at your school. The Virginia Department of Education (VDOE) has decided that there are certain skills that it wants you to have when you graduate high school. Therefore, it requires all students in Virginia to take the EOC exams in the core subjects: English, math, science, and history/social science. These exams evaluate not only what you have learned but also how well your school has taught its students.

What Exactly Is an SOL?

You've probably heard the EOC exams referred to as the "SOL tests." SOL stands for *Standards of Learning*, which is simply the name for the specific set of skills that the VDOE has earmarked for each core subject.

For example, in Algebra I, the Standards of Learning state that a student should be able to calculate a square root to the nearest tenth. So, rather than just taking your Algebra I teacher's word for it, the VDOE has drawn up its own Algebra I exam to make sure you can, in fact, compute a square root to the nearest tenth (among other skills). If you and enough of your classmates *can't* calculate a square root, the Board can point to the bad test results, and your high school is now in the hot seat. Sounds pretty good so far, right? I can hear you now: "I always knew there was something seriously wrong with my school . . . it's about time something was done . . . I knew that teacher didn't know what he was doing."

Sorry, the VDOE also plans to point a finger at *you*! Not only can schools lose their accreditation (read: financial support) for poor SOL test performances but (starting with the class of 2004) failures on the EOC exams can cost students their diploma. Yikes! It looks like you and your school are in this together.

If you want to know more about the VDOE standards, try its website:http:// www.pen.k12.va.us/ VDOE/Instruction/ sol.html

If you're feeling a little nervous (How *do* you compute a square root to the nearest tenth anyway?), don't sweat it. We're going to ensure that you have mastered every skill that the VDOE expects you to know for the Algebra I EOC test. We'll give you practice questions and explain the ins and outs of the test, and we'll explain how many questions you need to get right and how many SOL exams you need to pass in order to receive your diploma. In short, you've purchased the only guide to the Algebra I EOC exam you'll ever need. Congratulations for thinking ahead!

Who Is the Princeton Review?

We are the world's leader in test preparation. We've been preparing students for standardized tests since 1981 and have helped millions reach their academic and testing goals. Through our courses, books, and online services, we offer strategy and advice on the SAT, PSAT, SAT IIs, and the Stanford-9, just to name a few. And now we've set our sights on the Virginia EOC exams.

We Have the Inside Scoop

There's been a lot of hoopla surrounding the SOL tests over the past few years, and with so much at stake it's easy to lose sight of one basic fact—the EOC test is *only* a test. It is a standardized test for that matter, and like any standardized test, the Algebra I EOC exam is not immune to strategy and preparation.

We have made sure that every skill listed by the Standards of Learning is reviewed and practiced in this book.

All of the information that's been released regarding this exam is reflected in this book. We've been looking at standardized tests like the Algebra I EOC exam for years, and we'll share our special techniques to approaching standardized tests and mathematical problems so you'll have every possible opportunity to score your best on this exam.

One of the biggest obstacles for students in standardized testing is test anxiety. Taking the EOC exams with graduation on the line is like high-altitude training—the conditions couldn't be more stressful. In order to calm and prepare you for this exam, we've dedicated countless hours of research to help demystify the Algebra I EOC exam. In addition, we've written two practice tests to help you realistically evaluate your skills.

How Is This Book Organized?

This book has two primary purposes. First, we will familiarize you with the structure of the exam and recommend the soundest test-taking strategies to maximize your score. We're here to help—whether you want to earn advanced honors or just pass and get the heck out of Dodge.

Second, we want to make sure that you're familiar with the raw material of the exam—the actual algebraic concepts that must be mastered to do well on the exam. We will focus on exactly how the Virginia EOC exam tests your math skills so you will know what to expect on exam day.

Chapter 3 contains a basic algebra review to help you freshen up on some of the more elementary skills on the Algebra I EOC exam. It includes information on fractions, real numbers, and properties of numbers. If you're comfortable with the material in that chapter, feel free to skip it and move on to chapter 4. Chapters 4 through 7 contain detailed subject reviews that explain every skill-set the Algebra I EOC tests. This includes a complete review of the math skills that the VDOE wants you to have when you finish your Algebra I course.

Finally, chapters 8 through 11 include two complete practice exams with answer keys and explanations so that you can assess your skills under exam conditions. After you've been through this book, there will be no surprises when you take the actual Algebra I EOC test.

What Do the SOL Exams Mean for Graduation?

This is a big question, and we want to clear this up before we proceed to the finer points of how to ace this test. So, here's the skinny:

Starting with the graduating class of 2004, students must pass 6 of 12 possible EOC exams in order to graduate and receive a "standard" diploma. But hey, this is twenty-first century America—who wants to be plain old standard?

For all the gunners out there (and we hope you're one!), there's also an advanced studies diploma, which requires that you pass 9 of the 12 EOC exams. Regardless of which diploma you're shooting for, the Algebra I EOC test is the easiest math exam that earns credit toward a diploma. So it makes sense that you'd want to knock this test out as early as possible to help alleviate any anxiety the VDOE EOC exams process may create.

Let's look a little closer at the requirements for each type of diploma.

A Standard Diploma

In order to graduate, a student must pass 6 of the 12 SOL exams as follows: You need to pass both English exams, one math, one science, one history, and another EOC exam of your choice. Might as well start with Algebra I, eh? Here's a list of the 12 SOL exams that are offered.

Virginia EOC SOL Tests:

English: Writing

English: Reading/Literature/Research

Algebra I

Algebra II

Geometry

Earth Science

Biology

Chemistry

World History & World Geography to 1000 AD

World History & World Geography from 1000 AD to the present

U.S. History

World Geography

An Advanced Studies Diploma

The Advanced Studies Diploma is a fancier diploma obtained by, you guessed it, passing more EOC exams! To qualify for an Advanced Studies Diploma, you have to knock down an additional math, science, and history EOC test, as well as a few extra school courses.

For an Advanced Studies Diploma, you have fewer options. Because you can only opt out of three of the EOC SOL exams, the Algebra I test is an essential starting point.

Courses and SOLs Required for a Diploma

Subject	# of courses needed for HS Graduation	# of verified EOC tests needed for Standard Diploma	# of verified EOC tests needed for Advanced Diploma
English	4	2	2
Mathematics	3	1	2
Laboratory Science	3	1	2
History and Social Sciences	3	1	2
Health & Physical Education	2	0	0
Fine Arts or Practical Arts	1	0	0
Electives	6	0	0
Student Selected Test	0	1	1
Totals	22*	6	9

*For an Advanced Diploma, you will need 24 credits to graduate.

Frequently Asked Questions

* What's a Passing Score?

When you take an EOC exam, there are three possible outcomes: Fail, Verified Credit, or Advanced Proficiency. Verified credit, a credit you can apply toward graduation requirements, is obtained by answering a minimum number of questions correctly. Here's the big news: As of this printing, you need to get 27 correct answers out of the possible 50 (54 percent) to pass the Algebra I EOC exam.

Although this number is not set in stone for the upcoming exams, there's no reason to believe it will shift significantly. So, you now know approximately how many questions you'll need to get right.

* What if I Do Really Well?

The VDOE wants to recognize students who perform exceptionally well, so they've designated a score of "Advanced Proficiency." In order to earn advanced standing, you need to answer 45 out of the 50 scored items correctly (90 percent). This leaves little room for error.

* What are the Benefits of Advanced Proficiency or an Advanced Studies Diploma?

The most obvious benefit (besides rightfully basking in your own, obviously superior intelligence) is how it looks on a college transcript. College admissions get more competitive each year, and earning a special diploma for excellent test scores is the kind of gold star that could stand out on your application.

* When are the SOL Exams Offered?

With the exception of the English: Writing End-of Course SOL exam, the EOC tests are administered at the end of the fall and spring semesters.

Check your school calendar for specific testing dates in your school division. The EOC exams are also offered at the end of the Summer semester—for students attending summer school because of poor EOC exam performance (among other reasons). But we intend this book to help you avoid that scenario!

* How and When is the Algebra I EOC Exam Scored?

We hope this isn't too much of a shock, but your answer sheet is fed through a giant machine, and a final grade is spit out. What you may be more interested in is when you'll find out about your score—typically around six weeks after you take the test, with seniors receiving priority.

* What Happens if I Don't Pass Enough SOL Exams by Graduation?

Trouble. Despite grim results on the initial batch of SOL exams, there's no indication that the VDOE is going to back down from its SOL graduation requirements for the class of 2004. The current rules state that students who complete a prescribed course of study, but do not pass enough SOL exams, receive a **Certificate of Program Completion** in lieu of a diploma. So, unfortunately, the End-of-Course SOL exams now carry the two heaviest consequences that any high school student can imagine: summer school and not "walking" at graduation time.

*   What Does the Test Look Like?

The Algebra I SOL exam tests four major skill-sets called "Reporting Categories." Each evaluates specific algebraic concepts and skills. Later in the book we will review all the specific skills you'll need to master to succeed on the test. If you want to peek at them now, you can check out the VDOE website at www.pen.k12.va.us. We've dedicated about a chapter to each reporting category, and we will make sure that each is sufficiently explained.

The End-of-Course SOL Algebra I test (remember only 50 questions count) breaks down according to Reporting Category in the following way:

Reporting Categories (Skill-Sets)	# of Questions	Covered in the Book
Expressions and Operations	12	(chapter 4)
Equations and Inequalities	18	(chapters 4 & 5)
Relations and Functions	12	(chapter 6)
Statistics	8	(chapter 7)

Total # of Genuine Questions:	50
Field Test Items:	10
Total Questions:	60

*   What is a Field Test Item?

A Field Test Item is an experimental question that does not count toward your final score. Unfortunately, you have to answer it anyway. The test-writers use students' performance on these questions to determine whether they've written good questions for use on future exams. Since you have no way of knowing which questions are field tests and which ones actually count, work as if every question affects your score.

A History of the Test

The VDOE developed the SOL in an attempt to standardize its curriculum and ensure "quality control" among both teachers and students. The VDOE was concerned that students lacked fundamental reading and math skills and were inadequately prepared for high school and the job market. The first SOL exams took place in the Spring of 1998, with the stated goal of raising student achievement by holding both the student and educational system accountable to the results of the SOL exams. The results have been mixed, to say the least.

> The 40 percent of students who passed enough 1998 Spring EOC exams to qualify for graduation under the 2004 criteria is well below Virginia's current graduation rate.

Only 40 percent of the students who took the 1998 Spring SOL exams passed enough to qualify for graduation under the 2004 criteria. Though there have been modest gains since the first series of SOL exams, many diplomas are threatened by the requirements. Nevertheless, the VDOE still plans to implement its graduation requirements for the class of 2004.

We have designed this book to give you every opportunity to pass and excel on the Algebra I EOC exam. With the help of this book, the Algebra I EOC exam will not be the *end* for you.

Chapter 2

Strategies and Techniques

Whether you're gunning for an advanced proficiency mark, or just trying to nail down a verified credit for graduation, the EOC exams present a unique challenge that must be taken seriously. Relax, you've already taken an important first step: You decided to prepare. This book will help you score your best.

In this chapter, we introduce you to several very useful techniques that you can apply to any standardized math test—but specifically to the Algebra I EOC exam.

The techniques we describe over the next few pages will be critical in maximizing your score. It's important that you not only understand the techniques and strategies but also employ them properly. We've gained enough experience with exams like these to not waste your time with anything that's not crucial to your success. So let's buckle down and get to it!

Rules of the Game

In some ways, it's helpful to think of a standardized test like the Algebra I EOC exam as a game (granted, not a very fun one). Like any game, it plays by certain rules that are as important to the test as the actual skills it is designed to quantify.

Imagine the tallest, strongest, fastest, and most agile high school athlete in the world has been inserted into the starting lineup of your football team. This athlete has just moved from Luxembourg and has never played football before in his life. When he catches the kickoff, he runs straight for the sidelines where he grabs a water cooler and a cheerleader and darts directly out of the stadium, thinking he has won the game. Our fictional football player had the skills to be a good player, but he didn't understand the rules of the game. And in the same way, not understanding the rules of the Algebra I EOC exam can cost you just as dearly.

Two equally skilled Algebra I students could get very different scores if one tester understands the rules and the other doesn't. Let's take Max and Mary Smith and assume that they have similar algebra skills. Let's also assume that each knows the answer to 25 of the 50 test questions. Mary knows the rules, and since there is no guessing penalty, she bubbles in the remaining 25 questions, and gets 6 more answers correct. Max is not as well informed and leaves them blank. On the strength of her 6 correct guesses, Mary goes from a 25 to a 31, thereby passing the exam. Max, on the other hand, gets to go to summer school.

Granted, this is an extreme case, but it underlines the importance of knowing all the relevant rules to the test. Now that we've gotten your attention, here are the major rules to remember:

* **There is no guessing penalty!**

    Unlike some other tests, the Algebra I EOC exam does not penalize you for incorrect answers. This means there should be absolutely no blanks left on your answer sheet! If you're not sure how to answer a question, guess. If you can eliminate one or two answers, guess. If you've got a headache and you're not going to work out the last five questions, no matter what anybody says, guess.

*   The test is untimed.

Combined with the absence of a guessing penalty, this rule leaves no reason why you shouldn't finish the test. Take your time, and when in doubt, double-check any answers you're unsure of.

*   You can use a calculator, a ruler, and a formula sheet.

Being able to use a ruler and a four-function graphing calculator offers a tremendous advantage. We address how to use these tools to their fullest potential in the next section. Also, at the beginning of our practice tests, we provide a copy of the formula sheet.

Now that we've shared some important rules, let's look at some powerful tools that you can apply to your problem-solving approach.

The Process of Elimination (POE)

The exam's multiple-choice format affords some interesting opportunities that we'll show you how to take advantage of. For example, imagine a geography test in which you open the test booklet to find the following question:

What is the capital of Malawi?

Unsure? On a nonstandardized test, you'd have to guess, and you would probably be wrong. But on the EOC exams, you just pick the answer you think is best. Often, if we look closely at the answer choices, they provide us with valuable information. This is at the heart of all of our POE strategies. Let's take a look at the answer choices in our example.

Example 1

What is the capital of Malawi?

A   Paris

B   Lilongwe

C   New York

D   London

Do you think you could guess here? **A**, **C**, and **D** are all cities that you probably recognize are *not* the capital of Malawi. So, if your geography teacher stopped you in the hall and gave you a pop quiz, you would be stumped. But on a standardized test with a multiple-choice format, you can get it right! Singling out *Lilongwe* as the most likely suspect is an example of using Process of Elimination (POE).

POE works with math as well. Let's look at an example more in tune with the Algebra I EOC exam.

Example 2

What is the square root of 117, rounded to the nearest tenth?

F   100.8

G   10.8

H   1.1

J   0.1

Remember: The key to solving Algebra I test questions is attacking the answer choices.

There is the potential for a lot of calculation here, but it's unnecessary. The key is to attack the answer choices. Notice the large numerical difference between answer choices. Answers **H** and **J** are clearly too small and can be quickly eliminated. And **F** is way too big to be the square root of 117, meaning the only possible answer choice is **G**, which we arrive at without any calculation at all!

We've now demonstrated how powerful POE can be on a standardized test. Although it's rare that you'll be able to eliminate all three wrong answers, it *is* common to be able to cross out one or two. And since the test doesn't penalize you for bad guesses, POE can have a significant impact on your score. You should supplement your algebraic ability with smart test-taking and POE. Now we'll introduce a few more important techniques that you can apply to this test.

Backsolving

Backsolving can be used on algebra questions that have *real numbers* as answer choices. The test assumes that you'll try to solve everything algebraically, which is not always the most efficient way to solve a question.

To Backsolve, pick one of the two middle answer choices (**B** or **C**), and put the value back into the question. If the answer choice makes the statements in the questions correct, then you have the right answer. If not, you'll know to try another answer choice—and often whether that choice should be bigger or smaller. Since the answer choices are listed from smallest to greatest (when possible), picking a middle answer choice (**B** or **C**) first often eliminates extra wrong answer choices. This method also allows you to work and double-check the problem at the same time. Take the following question as an example:

> Real numbers that can be used for Backsolving include negative numbers, positive numbers, fractions, decimals, and zero. For example, $4x$ and $13y$, are *not* real numbers. See chapter 3 for a more detailed explanation.

Example 3

Which of the following is ONE solution to the following equation?
$$(x + 4)(x + 3) = 72$$

A −5

B 0

C 3

D 5

To Backsolve, simply pick one of the middle answer choices, say **C**, and put it back into the question. Think of it like this: If **C** is the right answer, then x should equal 3 and the equation should equal 72. Let's put 3 into the equation and see if we get 72:

$$(3 + 4)(3 + 3) = (7)(6) = 42$$

We got 42, not 72, which is significantly lower than what we needed. This information is still helpful because we now know the actual answer will need to be larger than 3—thereby eliminating answers **A** and **B**, leaving only **D**. Let's see if 5 works:

$$(5 + 4)(5 + 3) = (9)(8) = 72$$

Boom! When we Backsolve using 5 for the value of x, the equation comes out to 72. So, **D** must be the right answer—and we found it without doing one iota of algebra.

Backsolving is an excellent tool to fall back on when you are unsure of how to proceed on a question algebraically. In the case above, it is not only a safer way to solve the question (can you imagine the algebra?), but it is also much faster. We will show you not only the algebraic methods the test expects you to know but also instances in which Backsolving is helpful.

Let's try another example with a more complicated algebra question:

Example 4

What is the solution to this system of equations?

$$\begin{cases} y - 3 = 2x \\ \dfrac{8x + 2}{2} = y \end{cases}$$

F $x = -2, y = 10$

G $x = 4, y = 17$

H $x = 1, y = 5$

J $x = 4, y = 8$

The test asks us to solve this system of equations and presumes we will use our algebra skills. But like the previous example, this question has real numbers in the answer choice. Of course, you *could* use the system of equations to solve this question (covered in chapter 4), but first let's see how much easier it would be to Backsolve.

Start with answer choice **G**, and put its numbers, 4 and 17, back into the algebraic statements. When we use 4 for x and 17 for y, we find that the bottom equation works but the top equation does not—so **G** cannot be the right answer. Unlike the last question, we have no quick way of telling whether we want x or y to be larger or smaller, so we'll just pick another option. It's still faster than attempting to work the problem algebraically. When we put the values from answer choice **H** into the equation, notice that both equations are satisfied perfectly—making **H** the correct answer. How much easier was that than attempting the question algebraically?

Backsolving can significantly increase your accuracy and speed when solving problems. And more important, Backsolving offers another option if you get stuck attempting a traditional algebraic approach to a question.

> **Remember:** Backsolving can only be used when algebraic equation problems have answer choices with *real numbers*.

Plugging In

Plugging In is a technique which is very similar to Backsolving, insofar as it allows us to turn algebra into arithmetic. Instead of using real numbers in the original equation (as we do in Backsolving), we use variables. We simply take the variable or variables in the question and assign them actual numerical values. Then we can match these values with the answer choices. Let's take a look at an example:

Example 5

If $a = (3x - 4)$ and $b = (4y - x)$, then what is the value of ab?

A $\quad 12xy + 16y + 4x$

B $\quad 12x^2 - 16y - 4x$

C $\quad 12xy - 3x^2 - 16y + 4x$

D $\quad xy + 3xy - 16y + 4x$

First, let's assign values for x and y. Let's use 2 for x and 3 for y—it helps to use nice, solid integers. Plugging these values back into the question, we find:

$$a = (3(2) - 4) = (6 - 4) = 2 \text{ and } b = (4(3) - 2) = (12 - 2) = 10$$

When we multiply a (2) by b (10), we get 20, which we'll call our target number. Now we attack the answer choices. Keeping x as 2 and y as 3, let's see which answer choice successfully gives us our target.

A $\quad 12(2 \bullet 3) + 16(3) + 4(2) = 128$

B $\quad 12(2^2) - 16(3) - 8 = 12(4) - 16(3) = -8$

C $\quad 12(2 \bullet 3) - 3(4) - 16(3) + 4(2) = 20$

D $\quad (2 \bullet 3) + 3(2 \bullet 3) - 16(3) + 4(2) = -16$

Because answer choice **C** is the only one that gives the value of 20, we know it must be the right answer. Like Backsolving, Plugging In offers the advantage of working and double-checking the question—as well as saving you a lot of time. No matter how fast you are at doing algebra problems, you're faster at Plugging In and Backsolving.

Mnemonic Devices

Mnemonic Devices are techniques that can help you memorize things. In addition to using POE, Backsolving, and Plugging In to help find the right answers, mnemonics will help you remember specific algebraic skills and rules that will be vital for you to have when you take the Algebra I EOC exam. We've developed a few of them, and others you may remember from your Algebra classes. We want you to be familiar with all of them before we go into the subject review.

PEMDAS

PEMDAS is an acronym used to help you remember the order of operations for mathematical expressions. It's also helpful to remember this sentence: **P**lease **E**xcuse **M**y **D**ear **A**unt **S**ally.

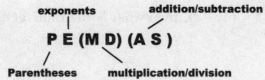

Knowing the proper order of operations is essential to solving most math problems on the Algebra I EOC exam. For example, you may be asked to solve the following equation:

$$4 + 8 \div 4 = x$$

You may be tempted to solve this problem such that $4 + 8 = 12$, then $\frac{12}{4} = 3$, so $x = 3$. But if you understand the rules of PEMDAS, you know that division gets solved before addition in an equation, so

$$4 + \frac{8}{4} = x$$

$$4 + 2 = x. \text{ So, } x = 6.$$

We discuss PEMDAS in greater detail in chapter 3, the math and algebra review.

If you're not familiar with the correct order of operations, you're in for a long day on exam day.

FOIL

FOIL is an acronym that stands for **First, Outside, Inside,** and **Last.** You may remember this term from your Algebra classes. It pertains to the order of operations when multiplying binomials, such as $(x + 4)$ and $(x - 5)$. Look at the diagram below to see how this operation is constructed.

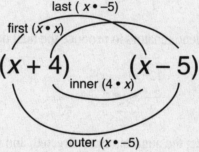

When we multiply the above equation through, we get the following result:

$$x^2 - 5x + 4x - 20$$

Notice that the two middle terms can be simplified, so the final result looks like this:

$$x^2 - x - 20$$

We'll review FOIL and more binomials in chapter 4.

The Bowtie

The Bowtie is a Princeton Review method designed to help you add or subtract fractions that don't have common denominators. Fractions can get complicated, and this mnemonic device should help simplify them. Take a look at the expression below:

$$\frac{4x}{1} - \frac{x}{3} =$$

Let's go through it step by step. First multiply up from the denominator (the bottom half) of the second fraction to the numerator (the top half) of the first:

$$\overset{12(x)}{\frac{4\,x}{1}} \overset{}{\nwarrow} - \frac{x}{3}$$

Then multiply the denominator of the first by the numerator of the second:

$$\overset{12\,(x) - (x)}{\frac{4\,x}{1} \times \frac{x}{3}}$$

Then multiply the denominators to produce the final denominator:

$$\overset{12\,(x) - (x)}{\frac{4\,x}{1} \times \frac{x}{3}} = \frac{}{3}$$

Then add or subtract the numerators as directed, and you're done!

$$\overset{12\,(x) - (x)}{\frac{4\,x}{1} \times \frac{x}{3}} = \frac{11x}{3}$$

Pretty easy, huh? Just remember this mnemonic and fractions will never give you trouble again!

Two-Pass System

Remember, to pass the exam you need around 27 correct answers (of the 50 "real" questions). Since you won't know which 10 of the 60 questions on the exam are field-test questions (and won't count), assume you'll need about 33 correct answers to pass.

If your goal is simply to pass the exam and move on, you should take comfort in the fact that you can temporarily skip over problems that are giving you a hard time. For this, we recommend a two-pass system—a system in which you look through the entire exam and answer the questions that you know and knock them out first. Since there's no guessing penalty or time constraints, you can always go back and battle with the more tricky problems.

However, if your goal is to receive an Advanced Proficiency mark, you have less room for error. To get the 45 questions required for this score, you need to be competitive on every question. This book prepares you for either goal.

Final Tips

It's important to note that the test has no significant order of difficulty. In other words, the Algebra I EOC exam does not get harder as you progress through the test (unlike the PSAT and SAT, which you may be familiar with). Also, note that the odd-numbered questions will have answer choices lettered **A**, **B**, **C**, and **D**, and the even-numbered questions offer choices **F**, **G**, **H**, and **J**.

Part II

Subject Review

Chapter 3

The Basics of Math and Algebra

In this chapter, we provide you with a quick overview of basic math rules and some of the unique words and symbols essential to your mastery of algebra. Once you grasp the material we present in this chapter you will be ready to delve deep into the realm of algebra.

> If you have any difficulty with the algebra skills introduced in this chapter, we recommend the book *Math Smart*, which explains this level of math in even greater depth.

Real Numbers

A detailed account of numbers isn't necessary here, so here is enough of the picture to allow you to make sense of how values are presented, and how you can compare them.

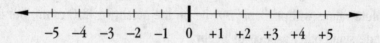

A number line, like the one above, extends forever in each direction and contains **positive** and **negative integers**, including zero. Integers are positive and negative numbers that are evenly divisible by 1—and zero. A few example of integers are, −41, −3, −1, 0, 19, 29, 301, and 420. A number's position on a number line represents its value. Positive integers are located to the right of zero and are greater than zero. The integers located to the left of zero are negative, and are considered less than zero. Zero is neither positive nor negative—it's just zero.

On the number line, as you move to the right (no matter where you start), the numbers get larger; and as you move to the left, the numbers get smaller. So, you can compare the size of any two numbers by locating them on the number line—the one that's farthest to the right is always the larger value. For instance, −25 sits farther to the right on the line; therefore, it is greater than −37.

Absolute Value

Because each space on the number line is of equal value, you can use it as a kind of ruler. Both 3 and −3 are a distance of three spaces from 0. When two distinct numbers, such as 3 and −3, are located the same distance from zero, they are called **opposites** (0 is its own opposite). The opposite of a positive number is negative, and the opposite of a negative number is positive.

The opposite of:	Is this value:	Stated matematically:
−3	3	$-(-3) = 3$
17	−17	$-(17) = -17$
0	0	$-0 = 0$

A number's distance from zero is its **absolute value**. Opposites always have the same absolute value—as you know, each one is the same distance (but in the opposite direction) from 0. Depending on the number, its opposite might be positive or negative, but its absolute value is *never* negative. Parallel lines situated on either side of a number depict absolute value; the absolute value of negative twelve looks like this:

$$|-12|$$

That's shorthand for: *How far from zero on the number line is −12?* The absolute value of −12 is 12. Absolute values will probably *not* be on the Algebra I EOC exam, but they're useful to help understand other aspects of algebra.

Comparing Values

Because the number line continues forever in each direction, any time you pick a value on the number line, an infinite number of larger or smaller values exist. Here are the standard symbols used to describe how values relate to one another:

Symbol:	Means:
=	*is equal to*
≈	*is approximately equal to*
≠	*is not equal to*
<	*is less than*
≤	*is less than or equal to*
>	*is greater than*
≥	*is greater than or equal to*

The first one is the standard *equals* sign you see in many equations, but the remaining five are **inequality** symbols.

$20 = 20$	20 is equal to 20
$6 \neq 14$	6 is not equal to 14
$4 > -20$	4 is greater than −20
$-8 < -3$	−8 is less than −3
$9 \geq 7$	9 is greater than or equal to 7
$3 \leq 3$	3 is less than oequal to 3

An inequality can be written in either direction. If $12 > 7$ (*12 is greater than 7*) is true, then you can also say that $7 < 12$ (*7 is less than 12*). It may help to think of the symbol as a Pac-Man that eats the larger number. We'll do some more work with inequalities in chapter 4.

> Some helpful terms to know: A *variable* is a number that is represented by a letter, such as x, y, or z; a *constant* is the figure that does not change in an equation; and a whole number is any non-negative integer (such as 1, 4, 20, or 121).

The Big Four (Operations)

Here's a table of all the terms involved in the different operations. Study them and we'll move on to a discussion of:

Operation	Operand(s)	Result
addition	addend	sum (or total)
subtraction	minuend, subtrahend	difference
multiplication	factor	product
division	dividend, divisor	quotient

In two of the four operations above, the order of the values you're working with doesn't matter. Whether you add 2 + 5, or 5 + 2, you'll always get the same result, and this is also true of multiplication, 2 • 5 yields the same value as 5 • 2. You'll notice that the table lists only a single operand name for each of these two operations, while subtraction and division both have two operands listed. The first value listed (for subtraction and division) must always be the starting value in either operation.

Subtracting Integers

Subtraction can initially seem kind of troublesome because of the way problems are usually worded. *"Subtract 7 from 12"* means start with 12, and take away 7. But here's something that might make things easier for you: *You can always turn subtraction into addition.* Instead of subtracting a value, you can always just *add its opposite*. Why would you want to do that? Well, changing subtraction to addition helps you avoid two trouble spots: 1) you won't have to worry about the *order* of the values involved, and 2) you won't need to worry about which value is larger and whether your subtraction involves *like* signs or *opposite* signs.

Instead of subtracting 7 from 12, you could just *add* the *opposite* of 7.

$$12 - 7 \text{ becomes } 12 + (-7)$$

When you get into the habit of changing all your subtraction problems into addition, you only need to remember two simple rules for the addition of signed numbers, noted in the section on Adding Integers on the next page.

Adding Integers

Any time you add two numbers, you are faced with one of two circumstances—both values will either have the same sign or the opposite sign. The following two rules take care of whichever combination you happen to run into:

1. *Addition with two like signs*

When you add two values that have *like* signs...

* add the absolute values of each of the two numbers

* the result receives the sign of the original values

2. *Addition with opposite signs*

When you add two values that have *opposite* signs...

* take the difference between the absolute values of the numbers

* the result receives the sign of the original number that had the largest absolute value

Let's take the subtraction problem above and turn it into an addition problem, and then apply the second addition rule to it. The word problem, *Subtract 7 from 12*, becomes, *Add −7 to 12*. Now, no matter how you write this sum (remember, order switching is allowed in addition), you'll get the correct answer:

$$-7 + 12 \text{ or } 12 + (-7)$$

Okay, so the absolute value of −7 is 7, and the absolute value of 12 is 12. The difference between the absolute values is 5, and since 12 has the larger absolute value and is positive, the result will be positive. When you add two values, the only rule you need to remember is this: *The sum gets the same sign as the number that has the larger absolute value.*

Multiplying Integers

When you multiply two values, you must follow rules to determine the sign of the product. You'll either be multiplying values that have the same sign (positive • positive or negative • negative), or values that have opposite signs (positive • negative or negative • positive). Here are the two rules used to determine the sign of the product:

Multiplication with like signs

When you multiply two values that have *like* signs…

* Multiply the absolute values of each of the two numbers

* The product is *always* positive

Multiplication with opposite signs

When you multiply two values that have *opposite* signs…

* Multiply the absolute values of each of the two numbers

* The product is *always* negative

Dividing Integers

Because division is closely related to multiplication, the rules for determining the signs of quotients are the same as they are for finding the signs of products. As in multiplication, division is done using just the absolute values of the two operands involved. Again, the result is determined separately, and follows the same rules as the product in multiplication problems. If the two values involved have the same sign (no matter what it is), the quotient is positive. If the two values have opposite signs, the quotient is negative.

Fractions

If you divvy up the spaces between the integers on the number line, you can cram in an infinite number of **fractions.** Fractions describe parts of a whole, and are in the form:

$$\frac{numerator}{denominator}$$

The **numerator** (the number on top) is the count of how many parts (or pieces) of the whole are involved, while the **denominator** (the number on the bottom) is a *non-zero* (that's important) integer that tells how many parts are needed to make up the whole. For instance, if a pie were cut into 6 pieces and 5 were served onto individual plates, 1 piece would be left. We express this with a fraction as $\frac{1}{6}$.

More on Fractions

All right, what do you need to know about fractions? Well, you need to be able to compare fractions the same way you compare integers. Adding (or subtracting) fractions is as easy as adding (or subtracting) whole numbers, as long as each denominator represents the same size whole.

Now let's choose two fractions and add them:

$$\frac{5}{8} + \frac{3}{8}$$

In this case, the fractions have the same denominator, also called a common denominator. When you add (or subtract) fractions with a common denominator, you add (or subtract) across their numerators, and the denominator stays the same. Take a look:

$$\frac{5}{8} + \frac{3}{8} = \frac{5+3}{8}$$

> **Remember:** You're never done with a fraction until you've *reduced* it to its lowest terms. When you reduce a fraction, you're looking for common factors in the numerator and denominator. The factor in this fraction is obvious; its 8, and the fractions can be reduced to 1.

We can now simplify the numerator:

$$\frac{5+3}{8} = \frac{8}{8}$$

Remember: Any fraction with a denominator of 1 can be rewritten with no denominator.

$$\frac{8}{8} = \frac{1}{1} = 1$$

Subtraction involving fractions with common denominators works the same way:

$$\frac{5}{8} - \frac{3}{8} = \frac{5-3}{8} = \frac{2}{8} = \frac{2(1)}{2(4)} = \frac{1}{4}$$

Adding and Subtracting Fractions Without Common Denominators

You won't always be lucky enough to be working with fractions with common denominators. How do you add or subtract fractions without common denominators? Simple, all you need to do is find a common denominator for them, and rewrite one (or both) of the fractions so they maintain their original values. Before we get to finding common denominators let's review fractions with equal values.

If a whole pizza starts out with eight pieces, half the pizza would have half that number, or four pieces ($\frac{4}{8}$); if it started out with six pieces, half would be three pieces ($\frac{3}{6}$). Finally, if half the pie is only one piece of pizza, that would be because the pizza was cut in two ($\frac{1}{2}$). So, we've just shown you three fractions which all express the same idea of half a pizza. Even though the fractions have different numerators and denominators, they represent equal values. Fractions rewritten to share a common denominator are called **equivalent** fractions. In the example we looked at before, near the middle of the solution you saw the fraction, $\frac{2}{8}$, which we simplified to $\frac{1}{4}$. In fact, there's an unlimited supply of fractions that are equivalent to $\frac{1}{4}$—here are just a few:

$$\frac{50}{200} = \frac{40}{160} = \frac{25}{100} = \frac{12}{48} = \frac{6}{24} = \frac{3}{12} = \frac{2}{8} = \frac{1}{4}$$

Okay, now suppose you wanted to add $\frac{1}{3}$ and $\frac{1}{6}$. Since these fractions have different denominators, you can't just go ahead and add them. If you have difficulty thinking up the common denominator, a quick way to find one is to just multiply the two original denominators—this might not give you the smallest common denominator, but it will work. If a fraction gets a new denominator, it needs a new numerator, too. The new fraction will *look* different, but it must keep its original value. The easiest way to add or subtract fractions without common denominators is by using the Bowtie Method, which we introduced in chapter 2. Let's go over it again quickly, just to make sure you understand it completely.

The Bowtie

We talked about the Bowtie in chapter 2, but it's a very important technique to help you with fractions. So we're going to review it again. Take a look at the expression below:

$$\frac{4x}{1} - \frac{x}{3}$$

Let's go through it step by step. First multiply up from the denominator of the second fraction to the numerator of the first:

$$\overset{12(x)}{\underset{1}{\frac{4x}{}}} - \frac{x}{3}$$

Then multiply the denominator of the first by the numerator of the second:

$$\overset{12(x) - (x)}{\underset{1 \qquad 3}{\frac{4x \qquad x}{}}}$$

Then multiply the denominators to produce the final denominator:

$$\overset{12(x) - (x)}{\underset{1 \qquad 3}{\frac{4x \qquad x}{}}} = \frac{}{3}$$

Then add or subtract the numerators as directed, and you're done!

$$\overset{12(x) - (x)}{\underset{1 \qquad 3}{\frac{4x \qquad x}{}}} = \frac{11x}{3}$$

Mixed Numbers

Mixed numbers combine an integer and a fraction into a single value. Although it might not look like it, a mixed number represents the addition of the integer part and the fractional part:

$$5\frac{2}{3} \text{ means } 5 + \frac{2}{3}$$

Remember: Any integer can be written as a fraction by simply putting it over 1.

You can handle this addition just as you would the addition of any two *unlike* fractions.

$$\frac{5}{1} \; + \; \frac{2}{3} = \frac{15}{3} \; + \; \frac{2}{3} = \frac{17}{3}$$

Any time you need to perform an operation that involves mixed numbers, first convert the mixed number into a fraction; this will make all your other calculations much easier.

Example 1

Lynn adds water to an aquarium that holds exactly $2\frac{1}{5}$ gallons. She added $1\frac{3}{4}$ gallons of water to fill the tank. How much water was in the tank before Lynn added any?

A $\dfrac{9}{20}$

B $\dfrac{11}{20}$

C $\dfrac{17}{20}$

D $1\dfrac{11}{20}$

Solution: You're looking for the difference between the tank's capacity and the amount Lynn added. But before you do anything, you'll need to convert the mixed numbers into fractions.

$$\overset{10}{\underset{1}{2}} \xrightarrow{+} \overset{1}{\underset{5}{1}} = \frac{11}{5}$$

$$\overset{4}{\underset{1}{1}} \xrightarrow{+} \overset{3}{\underset{4}{3}} = \frac{7}{4}$$

Now, if you subtract the amount Lynn added, from the tank's capacity, you'll know how much water was in the tank before Lynn added any.

$$\overset{44}{\underset{5}{11}} \xrightarrow{-} \overset{35}{\underset{4}{7}} = \frac{9}{20}$$

Here's a checklist for adding, subtracting, or comparing fractions:

* Change any mixed number(s) into fraction(s)

* Check the denominator of the fractions to be added, subtracted, or compared. If they're the same, continue with the next step. If they're different, find a common denominator

* *Add, subtract, or compare* just *the numerators of the fractions*

* Reduce any resulting fraction to its lowest common denominator

Multiplying Fractions

Multiplying fractions is easier than adding or subtracting them because we don't have to worry about common denominators. To find the numerator, you simply multiply the numerators, and to find the denominator you just multiply the denominators.

You're not done yet. Remember when we said that you were never done with a fraction until it was reduced to its lowest terms? Well, this is especially true when you're multiplying fractions:

$$\frac{4}{5} \cdot \frac{3}{10} = \frac{(4)(3)}{(5)(10)} = \frac{12}{50}, \text{ which we can reduce to } \frac{6}{25}.$$

There it is. Now here's a tip to save you some time. It's easier to reduce a fraction if you can look at some of its factors in the numerator and denominator. So let's do as much factoring out before we multiply as we can:

$$\frac{4}{5} \cdot \frac{3}{10} = \frac{(4)(3)}{(5)(10)} = \frac{2 \cdot 2 \cdot 3}{5 \cdot 2 \cdot 5}$$

Reducing becomes obvious. The factor of 2 in the numerator matches the 2 in the denominator. Cancel them out, and you're left with:

$$\frac{2 \cdot 2 \cdot 3}{5 \cdot 2 \cdot 5} = \frac{2 \cdot 3}{5 \cdot 5} = \frac{6}{25}$$

It's reduced, and you're done.

Let's do another one, just for fun.

$$\frac{9}{4} \cdot \frac{8}{21} = \frac{9 \cdot 8}{4 \cdot 21} = \frac{3 \cdot 3 \cdot 2 \cdot 2 \cdot 2}{2 \cdot 2 \cdot 3 \cdot 7}$$

The numerator and the denominator have been rewritten as products of the smallest factors we could find (this is called a **prime factorization**). Cancel out pairs of matching factors, and simplify.

$$\frac{(3 \cdot \cancel{3})(2 \cdot 2 \cdot 2)}{(2 \cdot 2)(\cancel{3} \cdot 7)} = \frac{3 \cdot 2}{7} = \frac{6}{7}$$

It's completely painless!

Dividing Fractions

Now, let's talk about dividing fractions. Any fraction division can easily be changed into multiplication; it's a snap. We said earlier that division in algebra is usually written using a fraction bar, but we'll make an exception here for clarity. Let's divide 51 by 17.

$$51 \div 17$$

Go ahead and write these integers as fractions, by putting each one over 1. Here's what it looks like now:

$$\frac{51}{1} \div \frac{17}{1}$$

To divide fractions invert the divisor (remember, the divisor is the value you're dividing *by*), and multiply the two fractions as we explained in the multiplication section above. Another way to say it is this: *Multiply the first fraction by the reciprocal of the second fraction.*

$$\frac{51}{1} \div \frac{17}{1} = \frac{51}{1} \cdot \frac{1}{17}$$

From here, you should already know what to do. The product of fractions is a single fraction with the product of the numerators as its numerator and the product of the denominators as its denominator.

Now reduce. (The answer is 3.)

Example:

$$\frac{4}{5} \div \frac{3}{10}$$

Solution: Just invert the divisor and multiply:

$$\frac{4}{5} \div \frac{3}{10} = \frac{(4)(10)}{(5)(3)} = \frac{40}{15} = \frac{8}{3}$$

Complex Fractions

Earlier we described a fraction as an integer numerator over an integer denominator, but the previous division example, as well as other division problems involving fractions, could also have been written as a **complex fraction**. A complex fraction is any fraction that has a fraction in either its numerator or denominator (or in both). Let's take a look:

$$\frac{9}{4} \div \frac{21}{8} \text{ can also be expressed as } \frac{\frac{9}{4}}{\frac{21}{8}}$$

> **Remember:** Any division can be turned into multiplication by just inverting the denominator and multiplying.

Scary-looking isn't it? Just remember to treat any scary-looking fraction by changing the fraction bar to division, and then simplify the terms.

$$\frac{\frac{9}{4}}{\frac{21}{8}} = \frac{9}{4} \div \frac{21}{8} = \frac{9}{4} \cdot \frac{8}{21} = \frac{72}{84} = \frac{18}{21} = \frac{6}{7}$$

Properties of Real Numbers

Now, let's get familiar with the properties of real numbers. It's unlikely that a question will test your knowledge of the precise terms, but understanding the following rules is essential to your ability to do well on the Algebra I EOC exam. Let's run through the relevant properties of real numbers and then we'll show you how the properties work in some sample questions. Get these rules down, learn how to identify properties of an equation, and solving the test questions will be a cinch.

Properties of Equality

Reflexive: $x = x$

The reflexive property of equality simply states that a variable can have one and only one value in an algebraic equation.

Symmetric: If $x = y$, then $y = x$

Transitive: If $x = y$, and $y = z$, then $x = z$

This is a very important property, allowing you to equate different unknowns in a series.

Substitution: If $a = b$, then b and a are interchangeable

Substitution plays a big part in our problem solving, allowing us to Plug In and Backsolve.

Addition: If $a = b$, then $a + c = b + c$, and $c + a = c + b$

Subtraction: If $a = b$, then $a - c = b - c$, and $c - a = c - b$

Multiplication: If $a = b$, then $ac = bc$ and vice versa

Division: If $a = b$ and $c \neq 0$, then $\dfrac{a}{c} = \dfrac{b}{c}$ and vice versa.

Properties of Addition and Multiplication

Commutative

Addition: $a + b = b + a$

Multiplication: $a(b) = (b)a$

Associative

Addition: $(a + b) + c = a + (b + c)$

Multiplication: $(ab)c = a(bc)$

Essentially, the associative property says that when deciding between addition or multiplication, the parentheses signs can be disregarded.

Additive Inverse (opposite): $a + (-a) = 0$ or $(-a) + a = 0$

Multilplicative Inverse (reciprocal): $a\left(\dfrac{1}{a}\right) = 1$, and $\left(\dfrac{1}{a}\right)\left(\dfrac{a}{1}\right) = 1$.

The multiplicative inverse or reciprocal is just a fraction flipped upside down. For example, the multiplicative inverse or reciprocal of $\dfrac{3}{2}$ is $\dfrac{2}{3}$, and vice versa. This rule states that any number multiplied by its multiplicative inverse is equal to one. For example, the multiplicative inverse of $2\dfrac{1}{2}$ is $\dfrac{2}{5}$, since $2\dfrac{1}{2}$ is equal to $\dfrac{5}{2}$.

Identity of addition: $(a + 0) = a$

Identitiy of multiplication: $(a \cdot 1) = a$

The identity property for addition and multiplication is fairly intuitive. For addition, any number plus 0 is equal to itself. For multiplication, any number times 1 is equal to itself.

Distributive of multiplication over addition: $a(b + c) = a\,(b) + a\,(c)$

$$a(b + c) = ab + ac$$

$$(b + c)(a) = ba + ca$$

You will most likely see the distributive property on your Algebra I EOC exam. In many algebraic situations, the distributive property allows us to distribute elements so that they can be divided. For example, consider the following equation:

$$17 (83) \bullet 17(17)$$

Some unlucky tester may multiply this out, when they could easily distribute the equation like so:

$$17 (83 + 17) = 17 (100) = 1,700$$

Consider yourself warned. The distributive property is helpful to know.

Equality Property Drills

Here are a few questions based on all of the properties that we listed above. If you can get these down, you'll be in great shape when you take the exam.

1   What is the multiplication inverse of $\dfrac{2a+3}{b}$?

    A $\dfrac{b}{2a+3}$

    B $\dfrac{5}{ab}$

    C $\dfrac{2}{3}ab$

    D $\dfrac{3}{2}ab$

Here's how to crack it:

Don't panic because you see fancy terms. An inverse (or reciprocal) is just a fraction turned upside down. **A** is the correct answer.

2   Which of the following is equal to 17 + 13, if a = 17 and b = 13?

    F $b + a$

    G $b - a$

    H $a - b$

    J $2(a + b)$

> **Remember:** A number times its multiplicative inverse always equals 1!

Here's how to crack it:

If you are at all in doubt, Plug In to each choice and determine which is equal to 30. **F** does it. This is an example of the commutative property of addition: $a + b = b + a$.

3   Given that $x = y$, which of the following is equal to $x - c$?

A $\dfrac{x}{c}$

B $y - x$

C $y - c$

D $x - y$

Here's how to crack it:

If there's any doubt, Plug In. This is the subtraction property of equality. The correct answer is **C**.

4   Which of the following expressions is equal to $w(x) + w(y)$?

F $x(y)w$

G $x(y + w)$

H $w(x + y)$

J $\dfrac{w}{(x + y)}$

Here's how to crack it:

Plugging In works just fine, if you're not sure. For example, if we say $w = 2$, $x = 3$, and $y = 4$, our initial statement, $w(x) + w(y)$ equals 14. Note that Plugging In these same numbers, only answer **H** gives us 14. Otherwise, you can factor out the w to get the answer.

Mathematical Order of Operations

All mathematical processes follow a standard order of operations which dictates which calculations receive priority when solving an equation with multiple operations. Let's make sure we remember what operations take precedence over the others so there will be no confusion when these problems appear.

PEMDAS (remember it from chapter 2?) is an acronym and a common mnemonic device (memory trick) for the order of operations: <u>**P**</u>lease <u>**E**</u>xcuse <u>**M**</u>y <u>**D**</u>ear <u>**A**</u>unt <u>**S**</u>ally. (It never was established just what it was that dear Aunt Sally actually did—use your imagination.) PEMDAS is essential to solving the majority of the questions on the SOL exam, so make sure it is second nature by exam day.

So, according to PEMDAS, we compute everything in Parentheses first (when there's more than one set of parentheses we go from inner parentheses out), and then we deal with any Exponents. We then Multiply and Divide (working from left to right), and then Add and Subtract (again, working from left to right). Note the parentheses in the above graphic. Since multiplication and division are essentially the same operation (i.e., dividing by 2 is the same as multiplying by $\frac{1}{2}$), one does not take precedence over the other. So we simply proceed from left to right.

For example, if we consider the statement $6 \div 3 \bullet 2$, is the answer 4, or is it 1? Because we move through the expression from left to right, we first divide 6 by 3, which gives us 2, then we multiply that by 2, and arrive at our answer, 4. The same holds true with addition and subtraction. They, too, are essentially the same operation (subtracting 2 is the same as adding -2), so we move through the expression from left to right when both addition and subtraction are involved. But, remember, we always multiply and divide before we add or subtract.

Those are the ground rules, so let's look at a few basic examples and make sure that the order of operations makes sense.

PEMDAS Drills

For more experience using PEMDAS, compute the following three problems.

1 $(6+3)^2 - 7 \cdot 3 = ?$

2 $\dfrac{17 \cdot 2 - 4}{5 + 3} = ?$

3 $\dfrac{7 + \dfrac{10}{2} - 8 \cdot 4}{8 - 3 \cdot 2}$

Solutions:

In problem 1 we first add 6 and 3 because they're in the parentheses, next we square the sum and the result is 81. Note that we must multiply 7 and 3 before we subtract from 81. 81 − 21 is 60, the correct answer.

Problem 2 requires us to multiply 17 times 2 (giving us 34) and then subtract 4 (giving us 30 on the top of the equation). Dividing by 8 (5 + 3) gives us $\dfrac{30}{8}$ as our answer, or $\dfrac{15}{4}$. The entire equation falls under the envelope of division, which is why we add 5 and 3 before dividing.

Problem 3 is similar, and the result is:

$$\frac{7 + 5 - 32}{2} = -10$$

Now that we've reacquainted ourselves with the order of operations, let's review how the actual exam tests you on it.

PEMDAS Questions on the Algebra I EOC Exam

The Algebra I EOC exam asks you to solve algebraic expressions that test your knowledge of PEMDAS. These questions are presented both in the standard equation form and as "verbal expressions," or word problems. By translating the words into simple mathematical operations and following the order of operations, these questions will be a breeze. Below we give you a couple of examples of both standard equation and word problems.

Example 1

What is the value of $3xy + 4 - y^2x$, if $x = 2$ and $y = -1$?

A   4

B   0

C   −4

D   −8

Here's how to crack it:

Plug in the values given for the variables and follow PEMDAS!

$$3xy + 4 - y^2x$$
$$3(2)(-1) + 4 - (-1)^2(2)$$
$$-6 + 4 - 2$$
$$-4$$

So, everywhere we see x, we Plug In 2, and everywhere we see y, we Plug In −1. The result is −4, so the correct answer is **C**.

Example 2

What is the value of $\dfrac{6x^2 + 3y - 1}{xy - 4}$, if $x = -3$ and $y = 1$?

  F   8

  G   0

  H   −4

  J   −8

Here's how to crack it:

Plug In and follow PEMDAS!

$$\frac{6x^2 + 3y - 1}{xy - 4} = \frac{6(-3)^2 + 3(1) - 1}{(-3)(1) - 4} = \frac{54 + 3 - 1}{-7} = \frac{56}{-7} = -8$$

The correct answer is **J**.

Example 3

If $\dfrac{1}{2}$ of x is equal to 18, what is x?

  A   9

  B   18

  C   36

  D   72

Here's how to crack it:

Translate and solve. $\dfrac{1}{2} \cdot \dfrac{x}{1} = 18$. Next, multiply to get $\dfrac{x}{2} = \dfrac{18}{1}$.

Then we can cross-multiply to get $x = 36$, or answer choice **C**.

Example 4

A certain actor demands that his salary be equal to $\frac{1}{5}$ of a movie's total revenue, plus $\frac{1}{2}$ of all the popcorn sold during the screening of his movie. If his movie generated $50,000 and $700 of popcorn was sold while his movie was playing, how much is the actor demanding to be paid?

F $5,125

G $10,350

H $20,700

J $41,1401

Here's how to crack it:

Read carefully (at the end of this chapter we'll give you some helpful hints on translating the words in word problems into operations) and Plug In! $\frac{1}{5} \cdot 50,000 = 10,000$,

and $\frac{1}{2} \cdot 700 = 350$. Add them together for 10,350. The correct answer is **G**.

Exponents

Exponents denote repetitive multiplication. For example, the expression 5^2 is equal to $5 \cdot 5$, or 25; 5^3 is equal to $5 \cdot 5 \cdot 5$, or 125. 5 is called the **base**, because it's the number that is repetitively multiplied, and 2 and 3 are called the **exponents.** They denote how many times we need to multiply the base by itself. Exponents can also be referred to as the *power* of a certain number. For example, 4 to the third power is another way of saying 4^3. Also, a number raised to the power of 2 is commonly referred to as that number "**squared**," and a number raised to the power of 3 is referred to as that number "**cubed**."

The laws of exponents can be confusing, so here are a few rules we'd like to review while we explore how exponents work. Keep in mind that these rules can be verified by simply expanding the expression out exponentially—we'll give an expanded example for greater clarification of each rule.

* **Rule for the Multiplication of Exponents:** $a^b \cdot a^c = a^{b+c}$

When multiplying exponents of **like base**, we need only **add** the exponenents together, like so:

$$3^3 \cdot 3^4 = (3 \cdot 3 \cdot 3) \cdot (3 \cdot 3 \cdot 3 \cdot 3) = 3^7$$

* **Rule for Raising an Exponent to a Greater Power:** $(a^b)^c = a^{b \cdot c}$

To raise an existing exponent to a further power, we multiply the exponents together. For example:

$$(3^3)^4 = (3^3)(3^3)(3^3)(3^3) = 3^{12}$$

* **Rule for Dividing Exponents:** $\dfrac{a^b}{a^c} = a^{b-c}$

As with the rule for multiplication, this rule only applies when dividing exponents of like **base**, so let's look at an example to see why.

$$\frac{3^5}{3^3} = \frac{3 \cdot 3 \cdot 3 \cdot 3 \cdot 3}{3 \cdot 3 \cdot 3} = 3^2$$

This rule is pretty easy to visualize, because if we divide the 3s that appear on both the top and bottom, we're left with only two 3s to multiply together on top of the equation.

* **Exponents to the Power of 0 and 1**

Any number to the power of 0 is equal to 1, and any number to the first power is equal to itself.

$$3^0 = 1$$
$$3^1 = 3$$

* **Negative Exponents:** $a^{-2} = \dfrac{1}{a^2}$

This will be a lot easier to understand with an example. If we divided 3^3 by 3^5, the law of exponential division states that we should get 3^{-2}, equaling $\dfrac{1}{3^2}$, or $\dfrac{1}{9}$. When we expand this operation out, the basis for the law becomes clear.

$$\frac{3^3}{3^5} = \frac{3 \bullet 3 \bullet 3}{3 \bullet 3 \bullet 3 \bullet 3 \bullet 3} = \frac{1}{3 \bullet 3} = \frac{1}{9}$$

So, all the 3s cross out from the top of the fraction, leaving us with 1, divided by the two 3s left over. This is important because a negative exponent does not result in a negative number. As with all the rules for exponents, expanding out the equation should clear up any confusion.

Exponents and Algebraic Expressions

In the above examples, we explored the rules of exponents with numerical examples, but you should be able to apply those rules to algebraic expressions—terms consisting of variables—as well. A monomial is a number (7), a variable (a), or the product of a number and a variable ($7a$), and the exam tests how you apply the rules of exponents to monomial expressions. Fortunately, by memorizing the rules of exponents, you've taught yourself everything you need to know to apply the rules of exponents to algebraic expressions. Before we look at algebraic examples, let's make sure that you understand exponents and the order of operations.

What is the difference between the following expressions?

$$3x^2$$
$$(3x)^2$$

A quick glance tells you that one has parentheses and the other does not. This difference has important implications. In the top term, only the x is squared, but in the bottom term both the 3 and the x are squared. The parentheses in the second term tell us to square the product of 3 and x. The result is two very different expressions from two very similar looking terms.

$$3x^2 = 3 \bullet x^2$$
$$(3x)^2 = 9x^2$$

also:
$$-x = -x \bullet x$$
$$(-x)^2 = -x \bullet -x = x^2$$

Okay, let's look at few algebraic examples with exponents:

Example 1 $\qquad 7x^2y \bullet 3x^3 =$

Example 2 $\qquad \dfrac{36x^4y^3}{9x^2y^2} =$

Example 3 $\qquad 4(x^3)^3 \bullet (2x^2)^4 =$

Example 4 $\qquad x^{-15} \bullet x^{15} =$

Example 5 $\qquad 13,784,578,485,749^0 \bullet x^2 =$

Solutions:

Example 1 $\qquad 21x^5y$

Multiply like terms together as so $7(3)x^2x^3y = 21x^5y$.

Example 2 $\qquad 4x^2y$

When dividing, subtract exponents of like base. 36 divided by 9 gives you 4, x^4 divided by x^2 equals x^2, and y^3 divided by y^2 equals y^1, or y.

Example 3 $\qquad 64x^{14}$

To take an existing exponent to a higher power (again, must have like base), we multiply the exponents: $4(x^3)^3 = 4x^9$. In the second part of the equation, everything in the parentheses is increased by the power of 4, giving us $(2x^2)^4 = 2^4 \bullet (x^2)^4 = 16x^8$. Multiply both parts together, and you get $64x^{17}$.

Example 4   1

When multiplying, we add the exponents, and $-15 + 15 = 0$, and any non-zero number to the 0 power $= 1$, so, our correct answer is 1.

> **Remember:** When multiplying exponents of like base, add the exponents.

Example 5 x^2

This is another tricky question. The huge number is to the power of 0, so it must be 1. 1 times x^2 is x^2.

Exponents and Scientific Notation

Scientists, being the crafty people they are, developed a system, called **scientific notation**, to express very large and very small numbers in a short amount of space. This wonderful invention is also a testing topic on the SOL exam. Rather than expressing the distance from the earth to Alpha Centauri as 2,000,000,000,000,000,000,000 miles, it is more common to express this distance exponentially through scientific notation—a much more convenient $2 \bullet 10^{21}$ miles. Scientific notation is an easy way to keep track of your zeros and/or your decimal places. In our above example, there were 21 zeros following the 2; rather than write all those zeros out, we just use scientific notation. The goal of scientific notation is to express only the distinctive digits of large numbers—like converting 7,500 into $7.5 \bullet 10^3$.

> If a number as a positive exponent, the decimal point, gets moved to the right; if a number has a negative exponent, the decimal point gets moved to the left.

$$7.5 \bullet 10^3 = 7.5 \bullet (10 \bullet 10 \bullet 10) = 7.5 \bullet 1000 = 7,500$$

Negative Exponents

If we had a very small number, say .0000453, we could convert this into scientific notation by counting how many decimal places we need to move to the right to express the number with more concise digits. In this case, if we move the decimal place over 5 spaces, we could rewrite the number as $4.53 \bullet 10^{-5}$. We can double-check this result by converting the number back into its decimal form and repeating the process.

$$4.53 \bullet 10^{-5} = 4.53 \bullet \frac{1}{10^5} = 4.53 \bullet \frac{1}{100,000} = .0000453$$

Division and multiplication of numbers expressed in scientific notation are the most likely operations to appear on the SOL exam. These questions can get tricky, but only when you lose track of your decimal place. The trick to multiplying and dividing numbers expressed in scientific notation is to strictly discriminate between the decimal number and the exponent. Look at the following example:

What is the product of $3.23 \bullet 10^4$ and 200?

First, let's convert 200 into scientific notation, which changes our expression into:

$$3.23 \bullet 10^4 \bullet 200 =$$
$$3.23 \bullet 10^4 \bullet (2 \bullet 10^2)$$

Think of our next step as simply combining like terms. Multiply 3.23 by 2, and 10^4 by 10^2, and our equation ends up looking like:

$$3.23 \bullet 10^4 \bullet (2 \bullet 10^2) =$$
$$3.23 \bullet 2 \bullet 10^2 \bullet 10^4 =$$
$$6.46 \bullet 10^6 \text{ } or \text{ } 6,460,000 \text{ } (answer)$$

Exponents and Scientific Notation Drills

1 $2.4(10^{-3}) \bullet 3.2(10^5) =$

2 $\dfrac{3.3(10^8)}{1.1(10^3)} =$

3 $\dfrac{5.5(10^{-3})}{2.5(10^5)} =$

4 $1.7(10^{12}) \bullet 350 =$

5 $\dfrac{3.2(10^9)}{1600} =$

Solutions:

1 $7.68 \bullet 10^2$

The key is to combine the like terms. $2.4 \bullet 3.2$ equals 7.68 and $10^{-3} \bullet 10^5 = 10^2$. Combine them to form the correct answer above.

2 $3 \bullet 10^5$

3.3 divided by 1.1 is 3, and $\dfrac{10^8}{10^3} = 10^5$. Combine them for the correct answer.

3 $2.2 \bullet 10^{-8}$

5.5 divided by 2.5 is 2.2, and $\dfrac{10^{-3}}{10^5} = 10^{-8}$. Remember to subtract exponents when dividing exponents with like base.

4 $5.95 \bullet 10^{14}$

1.7 times 350 equals 595, which you'll then need to convert into scientific notation. By moving the decimal place of 595 two places to the left, we rewrite the number as $5.95 \bullet 10^2$, and then combine the 10^2 and 10^{12} by multiplying them, resulting in the answer above.

5 $2 \bullet 10^6$

3.2 divided by 1,600 is .002, which we'll need to convert to scientific notation by moving the decimal place three places to the right—giving us $2 \bullet 10^{-3}$. Multiply this by our remaining 10^9 and you'll get the answer $2 \bullet 10^{-3}(10^9) = 2 \bullet 10^6$ above.

Square Roots

Although square roots have a positive and negative root (because, for example, both 3 and −3 times itself equals 9), you will only be responsible for the positive roots. So, as far as the EOC exam is concerned, the square root of 9 is just 3.

Square roots are actually one of the easiest parts of the SOL exam. A square root, in case you forgot, is the inverse of a number squared. 3^2 is equal to 9; the square root of 9, written $\sqrt{9}$, is equal to 3 or −3. Estimating square roots is easy, once you memorize a few perfect squares—numbers whose square roots are integers. It's not a bad idea to be familiar with the perfect squares of integers from 0 to 15 so you can make quick estimations—but of course there's always the calculator. Estimating square roots without a calculator is a pretty simple procedure—you just place the root in between two perfect squares. For example, $\sqrt{73}$ is between $\sqrt{64}$ (8 squared) and $\sqrt{81}$ (9 squared), so we know that the square root of 73 is between 8 and 9. In this case, $\sqrt{73}$ is about halfway between $\sqrt{64}$ and $\sqrt{81}$, so we can safely assume that the square root of 73 is about 8.5. When we plug this into our calculator, we find that our estimation was right; the square root of 73 is equal to 8.544. Your calculator will always be there to confirm any estimates you're not so sure about.

Perfect Squares 0–10

$$\sqrt{100} = +/-10$$
$$\sqrt{81} = +/-9$$
$$\sqrt{64} = +/-8$$
$$\sqrt{49} = +/-7$$
$$\sqrt{36} = +/-6$$
$$\sqrt{25} = +/-5$$
$$\sqrt{16} = +/-4$$
$$\sqrt{9} = +/-3$$
$$\sqrt{4} = +/-2$$
$$\sqrt{1} = +/-1$$
$$\sqrt{0} = 0$$

Radical Expressions

No, these expressions will not be starting a revolution in your town anytime soon. A **radical expression** in math is one that contains a square root, and the test may have a question that expects you to simplify the expression rather than estimate its value. Simplifying radicals is no big task; simply factor out any perfect squares that are inside the radical (the square root sign) and see what you come up with. For example, in $\sqrt{45}$, we can factor out 9 from 45 to rewrite the radical as such:

$$\sqrt{45} = \sqrt{9 \bullet 5}$$

Since we can take the square root of 9, that root comes out from the square root sign, giving us its final, simplified form:

$$\sqrt{9 \bullet 5} = 3\sqrt{5}$$

You can always check your solution with a calculator. In this case, the square root of 45 is about 6.7 when fed into a calculator, and when we check our simplified answer we find that $3\sqrt{5}$ is also 6.7.

Square Root Shortcuts

Since the square root Standard of Learning is primarily concerned with the estimation of square roots, we designed the drill below to illustrate some short cuts in square root estimation (using your calculator is a fine example). But square roots play a big role in factoring algebraic equations as well, so make sure you're solid with the concept.

Square Roots Drills

Estimate the following square roots to the nearest tenth.

1 $\sqrt{40}$

2 $\sqrt{65}$

3 $\sqrt{10}$

Express the following square roots in their simplest radical form.

4 $\sqrt{72}$

5 $\sqrt{108}$

6 $\sqrt{90}$

Solutions:

1   6.3

Use your calculator! 6.324 rounds down to 6.3.

2   8.1

Ditto for the calculator. 8.06 rounds up to 8.1.

3   3.2

3.16 rounds up to 3.2.

4 $\sqrt{72} = \sqrt{36 \bullet 2} = 6\sqrt{2}$

5 $\sqrt{108} = \sqrt{9 \bullet 12} = 3\sqrt{12} = 3\sqrt{4 \bullet 3} = 3 \bullet 2\sqrt{3} = 6\sqrt{3}$

6 $\sqrt{90} = \sqrt{9 \bullet 10} = 3\sqrt{10}$

Remember: $\sqrt{x} \bullet \sqrt{x} = x$ where $x \geq 0$.
If this is confusing, plug in real numbers
to verify.

Word Problems

Your Algebra teacher probably taught you the fundamentals of algebra, but there's another aspect to the Algebra I EOC exam that may not have been stressed in your class: the dreaded word problem. The key to doing word problems successfully is your ability to translate word problems into mathematical operations. To illustrate the similarities between word problems and algebraic expressions, look at the following two questions.

1   **If the sum of 4x and 7 is 6 less than the product of 2x and 4, what is the value of x?**

2    $4x + 7 < 2x(4) - 6$

What is the difference between these two questions? The obvious answer is that the second question is much easier to understand. Both questions ask you to solve the same equation; the first one describes the problem verbally and the second does so mathematically. Translating word problems into the correct mathematical equations can often be difficult. Fortunately, here are some keys to make the translation of word problems into algebra much easier.

*   A **sum** is the result of **addition**

*   A **product** is the result of **multiplication**

*   A **quotient** is the result of **division**

*   The **difference** is the result of **subtraction**.

Memorize these terms immediately (if you don't know them already). There are also some other key words that may not be as obvious as the terms above, but signal specific mathematical operations in word problems.

"Of " and "Is," "More" and "Less,"—and "What?"

Without exception, "**Of** " in a word problem means **multiply** and "**Is**" means **equal to**. You literally substitute a multiplication sign for "of " and an equal sign for "is." Also, keep in mind that the test may use "**more**" to indicate **addition** and "**less**" to indicate **subtraction**, as well. Finally, when the test uses the word "**What**," substitute a variable. On the EOC exam "What" often indicates the variable that the word problem will ask you to solve for. All of this seems simple enough, until you get hit with a question like this:

> **If 8 more than the product of 6x and 3 is $\frac{1}{2}$ of the quotient of 24 and 4, what is x?**

This is where the sheer volume of operations can be mind-numbing. The key to solving this type of question is translating the words into algebra one step at a time, like so:

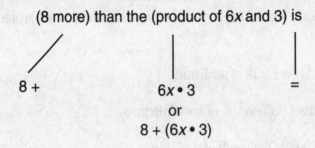

The "is" is the big daddy here, because it tells us where to equate—and now we have half of our equation. Let's look at the other half.

$$\text{is }(\tfrac{1}{2}\text{ of the quotient of 24 and 4).}$$
$$= \qquad \frac{1}{2} \cdot \left(\frac{24}{4}\right)$$

So the entire equation translates into this:

$$8 + 18x = \frac{1}{2}\left(\frac{24}{4}\right)$$

Solve it:

$$8 + 18x = \frac{1}{2}\frac{24}{4}$$

$$8 + 18x = \frac{1}{2}(6)$$

$$8 + 18x = 3$$

$$18x = -5$$

$$\frac{18}{18}x = -\frac{5}{18}$$

$$x = -\frac{5}{18}$$

Word Problems Drills

Let's try a few quick examples of word problems that also tests our knowledge of PEMDAS, and we'll be ready to start our review of linear equations and inequalities.

1   **Every time Patty goes shopping, she spends three times as much money as she earned that day at her waiting job. If Patty goes shopping and spends $600 on shoes—how much money did she make waiting tables that day?**

    A $200

    B $400

    C $600

    D $1800

Here's how to crack it:

Translate the words into algebra. The problem says that she spends three times as much as she makes, which we express as $3(earn) = spend$. The problem states she spent $600 on shoes, so the equation reads $3e = \$600$. We divide by 3 to arrive at the correct answer of $200, or **A**.

2　If the Boston Marathon is approximately $7.6 \bullet 10^4$ inches long, how many total feet are there in the Marathon? (Note, 12 inches to a foot).

F　$.63\overline{3} \bullet 10^3$

G　$6.3\overline{3} \bullet 10^3$

H　$63.\overline{3} \bullet 10^3$

J　$633 \bullet 10^3$

Here's how to crack it:

Remember to keep track of the decimal place! When we divide 7.6 by 12, we get $.63\overline{3}$. Combining this with 10^4, we get $.633 \bullet 10^4$. The test moved the decimal place to the right, meaning our exponent will get smaller by exactly one place, becoming $6.3\overline{3} \bullet 10^3$, or choice **G**.

3　A certain computer can make $1.7 \bullet 10^5$ calculations per second. At this rate, how many calculations will the computer make in $3.4 \bullet 10^7$ seconds?

A　$5.78 \bullet 10^2$

B　$5.78 \bullet 10^{\frac{5}{7}}$

C　$5.78 \bullet 10^{12}$

D　$5.78 \bullet 10^{35}$

Here's how to crack it:

Multiply each like term: 1.7 • 3.4 is 5.78. Then remember the rules of exponents. We add exponents when multiplying exponents of like base, giving us **H** and not **J**.

As we introduce more concepts later in the book, we'll continue to throw in word problems to keep you on your toes. Now let's go on to chapter 4: Equations and Inequalities!

Equations and Inequalities

Solving Linear Equations

Understanding linear equations is the first step on the Algebra I battlefield. Remember your algebra class (if that's possible), and you may recall that a linear equation is an equation that, when graphed, produces a straight line. We'll *graph* linear equations later. For now, the important thing to remember is that a linear equation is an equation that contains no exponents or square roots. Linear equations are the building blocks of all algebraic reasoning, and we're going to make sure you're comfortable with manipulating and solving them.

> A linear equation is an equation that contains no exponents or square roots.

Let's take an example of a simple linear algebraic equation so that we can outline the basic steps for solving it: $3x + 4 = 19$.

The goal in this example is to solve for the variable x. This means we need to isolate the variable from the rest of the equation. The first step, therefore, is to get rid of the 4 on the left side of the equation. Since we need to subtract 4 from the left side (to isolate our variable), we must also subtract 4 from the right side of the equation. The result should look like this:

$$3x + 4 = 19$$
$$\underline{-4 \quad -4}$$
$$3x = 15$$

Although we now have the variable x isolated on one side, we only know what is equal to $3x$. To solve for the single variable x, we must divide *both* sides by 3. When we do so, our final result looks like this:

$$\frac{3x}{3} = \frac{15}{3}$$

$$x = 5$$

Remember: Whatever you do to one side of the equation, you *must* do to the other.

So x is equal to 5. Notice that if you plug 5 back into the original equation, it solves for 19 perfectly—confirming that we have found the right answer. In the above example, we solved the equation using both subtraction and division to arrive at our value for x.

Solving Linear Equations with Fractions

Linear equations can get more complicated than the above example, especially when fractions are thrown into the equation. Hopefully, our review in chapter 3 prepared you for this. Let's look at a linear equation that has a fraction:

$$\frac{5}{3}x - 6 = 24$$

Note that our task here is essentially the same as it was in our previous example. We still need to isolate x, and we do it by performing the same operations to both sides. In this case, add 6 to both sides in order to isolate our variable:

$$\frac{5}{3}x - 6 = 24$$
$$\underline{+6\ \ +6}$$
$$\frac{5}{3}x = 30$$

We now have the x isolated, but we still need to figure out what number x actually

represents. In this case, the quickest way to solve for x would be to *multiply* both sides by

the *reciprocal*, or the inverse, of $\frac{5}{3}$.

$$\left(\frac{3}{5}\right)\frac{5}{3}x = 30\left(\frac{3}{5}\right)$$
$$x = \frac{90}{5}$$
$$x = 18$$

> **Remember:** The reciprocal of a fraction is just the fraction flipped over.

Excellent! Now let's look at more complicated linear equations. The test-makers will expect you to solve equations that have variables on both sides of the equation, as well as equations that use grouping symbols (such as parentheses and brackets). Here is an example of a linear equation with variables on both sides:

$$\frac{3}{5}x - 4 = x + 3$$

Although this equation has variables on both sides of the equation, our two fundamental rules still apply: (1) Isolate the variable (by subtracting like terms) and (2) solve for x. In this case, isolating the variable will involve manipulating one of the variables. We need to subtract x—and add 4—from both sides of the equation to isolate x.

$$\frac{3}{5}x - 4 = x + 3$$
$$\underline{-x + 4 \quad -x + 4}$$
$$-\frac{2}{5}x = 7$$
$$\left(-\frac{5}{2}\right)\left(-\frac{2}{5}x\right) = 7\left(-\frac{5}{2}\right)$$
$$x = -\frac{35}{2} = 17.5$$

Grouping Symbols

There are a few important rules regarding grouping symbols and linear equations. Of course you have to know PEMDAS, but make sure you know the following rules as well.

* Any grouped operations should be computed first.

* When dealing with more than one group in an equation, operations should progress from the inner group to the outer groups.

* When a variable is grouped with a number, you need to multiply the group out.

Take the following example:

$$3(y - 4) = y(13 + 2)$$

To simplify the equation, we multiply both elements that are grouped in the parentheses by the elements outside.

$$3(y - 4) = y(13 + 2)$$
$$3(y) + 3(-4) = y(13) + y(2)$$
$$3y - 12 = 13y + 2y$$

Now that we've simplified the equation, our job is to isolate and solve the variable, like in the previous examples. In this case, we only need to combine $13y$ and $2y$, then subtract $3y$ from both sides of the equation, as such:

$$3y - 12 = 15y$$
$$\underline{-3y \qquad -3y}$$
$$-12 = 12y$$
$$-1 = y$$

Solving Linear Inequalities

Inequalities are used for a range of possible variables (rather than a specific variable), with the equal sign (=) in the equation replaced by either a greater than (<) or less than (<) sign. Additionally, when the range of values includes the upper and lower limits, a bar is placed below the above signs to signify greater than or equal to ($\geq$) and less than or equal to ($\leq$). To solve linear inequalities, you follow all the rules as you do with linear equations, with one major addition: When you divide or multiply by a negative number to solve for the variable, you *must* flip the sign!

> **Remember:** Reading from left to right, the arrow (<, $\leq$ or $\geq$, >) will always point to the smaller value. It may help to think of the arrow as a Pac-Man that eats the larger number.

Let's look at an example to make these points a little clearer:

$$3(x - 3) < 7x + 4$$

We begin by multiplying through the parentheses sign, since it's our first priority.

$$3x - 9 < 7x + 4$$

Next, we're going to subtract $7x$ and add 9 from both sides to isolate our variable.

$$3x - 7x - 9 < 7x - 7x + 4$$
$$\frac{+9 \qquad\qquad +9}{-4x < 13}$$

In order to completely solve for this inequality, we have to divide both sides by negative 4, meaning that we'll have to flip the sign. This is the one important difference between solving inequalities and linear equations.

$$\frac{-4}{-4}x < \frac{13}{-4}$$
$$x > -\frac{13}{4}$$
$$x > -3\frac{1}{4}$$

With the sign flipped, notice that our result is exactly the same as if we had subtracted $3x$ and 4 from each side instead.

$$3x - 9 < 7x + 4$$
$$\frac{-3x - 4 \quad -3x - 4}{-13 < 4x}$$
$$\frac{-13}{4} < \frac{4x}{4}$$
$$-3\frac{1}{4} < x$$

Remember: When you divide by a negative number to solve for the variable, you *must* flip the sign!

So, no matter how you attempted to isolate x, you still get the same answer (x is greater than $-\frac{13}{4}$). Inequalities present no great difficulty if you just remember to flip the sign if multiplying or dividing by a negative number.

Inequalities and Range

Inequalities can also be used to express a range of values for a given variable. These expressions operate under the same rules for solving linear equations. For example:

$$-34 < 4x + 2 < 18.$$

We know that the equation $4x + 2$ falls between -34 and 18. The test will often ask for the range of x only, meaning that we need to simplify this inequality. All we have to do is subtract 2 from all sides of the inequality and then divide by 4.

$$
\begin{array}{c}
-34 < 4x + 2 < 18 \\
\underline{-2 \qquad -2 \ -2} \\
-36 < 4x < 16 \\
-\dfrac{36}{4} < \dfrac{4x}{4} < \dfrac{16}{4} \\
-9 < x < 4
\end{array}
$$

So, x must be larger than -9 and smaller than 4 in order to fulfill the inequality. These kinds of questions only get tricky because there is more than one inequality sign. However, the rules remain the same: ***Whatever you do to one side, do to the others.***

Linear Equations and Word Problems

Questions on the Algebra I EOC exam may ask you to Plug In specific values for a given equation. These can be handled with the same principles as solving linear equations. In some ways they're even easier—they can always be confirmed by Plugging In. Although word problems can be complicated at first glance, they can always be broken down into simple equations. Let's take a look at a question that might appear on your Algebra I EOC exam.

Example 1

If the formula for distance is expressed as $d = (r)(t)$ where d is distance, r is rate and t is time, how long would it take a car to travel 330 miles if it is traveling at 60 miles per hour?

    A   4.0 hours

    B   4.5 hours

    C   5.0 hours

    D   5.5 hours

Here's how to crack it:

This is simply a matter of plugging numbers into the formula and solving for the given value using the algebra skills we reviewed above. You should have formed an equation like so:

$$330 = 60t$$

To solve for t, we need only divide both sides by 60.

$$\frac{330}{60} = \frac{60}{60}t$$

$$5.5 = t$$

The correct answer is **D**.

Final Notes on Linear Equations

Make sure that you're confident in your ability to isolate and solve for a single variable equation. If you still have questions about them, be sure to seek help from your teacher. The ability to solve linear equations is essential to pass the EOC Algebra I exam. Let's look at different kinds of questions you can expect to see on it. More important, let's see if we can find any shortcuts!

Linear Equations Drill

1 If $4 < \frac{1}{4}(k+5) \leq 8$, which of the following answer choices represents the range of **k**?

A $8 < k \leq 27$

B $11 < k \leq 27$

C $16 < k \leq 32$

D $16 < k \leq 27$

Here's how to crack it:

Parentheses always take precedence, so we need to multiply $\frac{1}{4}$ by $(k + 5)$, leaving us with $4 < \frac{1}{4}k + \frac{5}{4} \leq 8$. To find **k**, we need to multiply the *entire* inequality through by 4, which leaves us with $16 < k + 5 \leq 32$. Again, whatever we do to one side, we do to the other, so when we subtract 5, we're left with **B**.

2 For the equation $7(x+3) - 3x = \frac{2}{3}x + 2$, what does **x** equal?

F   −63.33

G   −5.7

H   5.7

J   63.33

Here's how to crack it:

There are two options here. The first is to simply run through the algebra using the various rules we've spelled out above.

$$7(x+3)-3x=\frac{2}{3}x+2$$

$$7x+21-3x=\frac{2}{3}x+2$$

$$4x+21=\frac{2}{3}x+2$$

$$4x-\frac{2}{3}x+21=\frac{2}{3}x-\frac{2}{3}x+2$$

$$\underline{-21-21}$$

$$3\frac{1}{3}x=-19$$

$$\frac{10}{3}x=-19$$

$$\frac{3}{10}(\frac{10}{3}x)=-19(\frac{3}{10})$$

$$x=\frac{-57}{10}$$

$$x=-5.7$$

This requires a lot of algebraic steps, eh? So let's not forget to use our favorite test-taking strategy, **Backsolving**. As with any problem that asks you to solve with algebra and provides real numbers in the answer choices, working the algebra is purely voluntary.

$$7(x+3)-3x=\frac{2}{3}x+2$$

$$7(-5.7+3)-3(-5.7)=\frac{2}{3}(-5.7)+2$$

$$7(-2.7)+17.1=-3.8+2$$

$$-1.8=-1.8$$

By attacking the answer choices and substituting them for the variable x, we find that only **G** makes both sides of the equation equal. Therefore, it must be the right answer. Wasn't that quicker than the algebra? Even if you don't try the correct answer first for Backsolving, it's usually faster. Don't forget to use your calculator to crunch the awkward numbers.

3   A shoe company determines the price of each pair of its sneakers with the following formula: $p = 5(l + m + a) + 50$

Where p is the price, l the labor cost, m the material cost, and a is the advertising cost for each shoe.

What is the cost of a shoe whose material costs are $1.50 per shoe, labor costs are $1.50 per shoe and whose advertising costs are $20.00 per shoe?

A $139

B $150

C $165

D $250

Here's how to crack it:

No magic is required here. Just plug the numbers they give you into the equation, and follow your order of operations (always work through your parentheses first). $5(1.5 + 1.5 + 20) + 50 = 5(23) + 50 = 165$. You should get $165, or **C**.

4 A basketball player has a contract stipulation that his weight must satisfy the following condition: $801 < 3w - 6 < 1200$.

Which of the following inequalities satisfies this condition?

F $269 < w < 400$

G $267 < w < 402$

H $269 < w < 402$

J $270 < w < 401$

Here's how to crack it:

Simply add 6 to both sides and then divide by 3.

$807 < 3w < 1206$ is equal to **H**. Pretty easy, huh?

Polynomials

Algebraic expressions may contain multiple terms, such as $5x^2 + 16x + y$, or $2 + xy$. These terms are called polynomials, and the test will expect you to know how to manipulate them. We'll start this section with a review of the key terms you'll need to know to get the most out of our explanations.

* A **monomial**, if you remember from the last section, is an algebraic expression that is a number, a variable, or a combination of both. For example, $7, y, 5x$, and xy are all examples of monomials.

* A **binomial** is two monomials added or subtracted together, such as $5x + 4y$, or $17xy - 13zy$.

* A **trinomial** is three monomials added or subtracted together, such as $5x + 4y - 2z$

* A **polynomial** is the sum of two or more different monomials. So, note that a polynomial could be a binomial, or it could have even more terms in the expression. $7 + xy$ and $5x^2 + 16x + y$ are both examples of polynomials, although the first expression is also a binomial. We mention the difference because the exam may specifically refer to a binomial.

Some questions on the EOC exam will ask you to add, subtract, multiply, and divide polynomials, but don't worry, this isn't as complicated as it may sound.

Adding and Subtracting Polynomials

To add or subtract a polynomial, we must focus on **like terms**, or monomials within the expression that are identical except for their coefficients. For example, $7x$ and $5x$ would be considered like terms, as would $17xyz^2$ and $-9xyz^2$, for they only differ in their coefficient—the number before the variable. This may sound like gobbledygook, but terms like polynomial and monomial are just fancy ways to describe algebraic maneuvering that is actually pretty basic.

Like terms, such as the ones listed above, can be added or subtracted by their coefficients to create a much more concise expression. If they differ in any way outside of the coefficients, they can't be simplified. Period.

Spot and combine the like terms in the expression that follows:

$$17xy^2 + 4x + 5y - 16xy^2 - 6z + 5xy + 7z + xy - 4x$$

This can look scary, but once we reorder the equation according to its like terms, it will seem a lot easier. In order to reorder the equation, we must put all of the like terms next to one another, moving left to right through the equation.

$$17xy^2 - 16xy^2 + 4x - 4x + 5y - 6z + 7z + 5xy + xy$$

Now we need to combine the like terms, which, as mentioned above, consists of simply adding or subtracting the coefficients of the similar terms. Our final expression should look like this:

$$xy^2 + 5y + z + 6xy$$

Multiplying Polynomials

Remember this?

$$a(b + c) = ab + ac$$

This is the distributive property—the bread and butter in the multiplication and division of polynomials. The goal of multiplying and dividing polynomials is to restate the expression in its simplest form, and this often involves manipulating the expression using the distributive property. Complicated monomials are just singular terms that can be manipulated with the distributive property. For example, if we're multiplying $4x - y$ by $5xy$, we can use the distributive property to simplify the expression into one binomial. First, we multiply $5xy$ times $4x$ and then $-y$ as so:

$$5xy(4x - y) = 5xy(4x) - 5xy(y) \qquad \text{(Distributive Property)}$$

From here, we just need to multiply the like terms together as so:

$$5xy(4x) - 5xy(y)$$
$$20x^2y - 5xy^2$$

This is as simplified as this expression is going to get, because there are no more like terms to combine (x^2y and xy^2 are unlike terms and can't be combined; the exponents and the variables must match exactly). The test will also want us to factor polynomials by their greatest common monomial factor—the greatest terms we can take from both parts of the binomial—which, in this case, is $5xy$.

When multiplying polynomials, the distributive property is still the key—only now there is more than one term that we'll need to multiply through the other algebraic expression. Let's say we wanted to multiply $(2x - 3y)(4x + 3y - 7)$, our basic goal remains the same: to multiply every term in the first parentheses by every term in the second parentheses. To do this, we must break up the equation according to the distributive property:

$$(2x - y)(4x + 3y - 7) = 2x(4x + 3y - 7) - y(4x + 3y - 7)$$

All we've done is taken both parts of our binomial ($2x$ and $-y$) and multiplied them with the other equation—just like we did with our monomial. All that's left now is to multiply through both expressions:

$$2x(4x + 3y - 7) - y(4x + 3y - 7)$$
$$8x^2 + 6xy - 14x - 4xy - 3y^2 + 7y$$

For convenience, we'll reorder the expression emphasizing like terms, then simplify.

$$8x^2 - 3y^2 + 6xy - 4xy - 14x + 7y$$

Leaving us with the final expression:

$$8x^2 - 3y^2 + 2xy - 14x + 7y$$

Note that our only like terms were the $6xy$ and the $4xy$, but there can be many more in an equation. Let's look at a few examples utilizing the distributive property:

Use the distributive property to multiply the following expressions:

1 $4x(3xy + 4)$

2 $2x^2(3xy - 2x + 3)$

3 $(2x + 3)(5x + 4y - 12)$

4 $(-3x + 2y)(6x + 3y - 6)$

5 $(3x + 3xy)(4x - 4y + 3)$

> **Remember:** If any of these drills stump you, all you need to do is apply the distributive property. An algebreic term need not only be a single variable. As long as the variables are only multiplied or divided, it's considered a term. For example, $a(b + c) = ab + ac$, but the following expression also follows the distributive property: $(abc + def)(ghi + jkl) = abc(ghi + jkl) + def(ghi + jkl)$. Hope this helps!

1
$$4x(3xy+4) =$$
$$4x(3xy) + 4x(4) =$$
$$12x^2y + 16x$$

2
$$2x^2(3xy - 2x + 3) =$$
$$2x^2(3xy) + 2x^2(-2x) + 2x^2(3) =$$
$$6x^3y - 4x^3 + 6x^2$$

3
$$(2x+3)(5x+4y-12)$$
$$2x(5x+4y-12) + 3(5x+4y-12)$$
$$10x^2 + 8xy - 24x + 15x + 12y - 36$$
$$10x^2 + 8xy - 9x + 12y - 36$$

4
$$(-3x+2y)(6x+3y-6) =$$
$$-3x(6x+3y-6) + 2y(6x+3y-6) =$$
$$-18x^2 - 9xy + 18x + 12xy + 6y^2 - 12y =$$
$$-18x^2 + 6y^2 + 3xy + 18x - 12y$$

5
$$(3x+3xy)(4x-4y+3) =$$
$$3x(4x-4y+3) + 3xy(4x-4y+3)$$
$$12x^2 - 12xy + 9x + 12x^2y - 12xy^2 + 9xy =$$
$$12x^2 + 12x^2y - 12xy^2 - 3xy + 9x$$

FOIL (Multiplying a Binomial by a Binomial)

The distributive property can be simplified even further when multiplying a binomial by a binomial by memorizing a process called **FOIL**. We mentioned this mnemonic in chapter 2, but this process is extremely important to know. FOIL describes the order in which we combine the terms of one binomial with the other, by multiplying the **F**irst, **O**uter, **I**nner, and **L**ast terms together, and then combining the like terms. Let's look at two binomials and see how FOIL helps us combine them through multiplication.

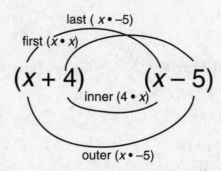

It actually makes no difference in what order you combine the terms as long as each term in the first parentheses is multiplied by each term in the second parentheses. When we multiply the above equation through, we get the following results:

$$x^2 - 5x + 4x - 20$$

And we notice the like term in the middle, which can be simplified as so:

$$x^2 - x - 20$$

This gives us the expression in its simplest form. Remember, there is no real difference between FOIL and the distributive property, and the primary usefulness of FOIL is that it's a little more efficient than Plugging In to the distributive property. Since FOIL is such an important skill, we'd like to reinforce it with a few practice examples.

> FOIL describes the order in which we combine the terms of two binomials: Multiply the **F**irst, **O**uter, **I**nner, and **L**ast terms together, then combine the like terms.

FOIL Drills

Simplify by using FOIL:

1 $(2x + 3)(3x + 4)$

2 $(x - 1)(x + 1)$

3 $(3x + 2)(2y - 3)$

4 $(x + 5)(y - 1)$

Solutions:

1
$$(2x + 3)(3x + 4) =$$
$$6x^2 + 8x + 9x + 12 =$$
$$6x^2 + 17x + 12$$

2
$$(x - 1)(x + 1) =$$
$$x^2 + x - x - 1 =$$
$$x^2 - 1$$

3
$$(3x + 2)(2y - 3) =$$
$$6xy - 9x + 4y - 6$$

4
$$(x + 5)(y - 1) =$$
$$xy - x + 5y - 5$$

Dividing Polynomials

In some instances, the distributive property will also allow us to divide polynomials. The key is to distribute out a common factor that a monomial divisor divides into evenly. To divide $5x + 15$ by 5, for example, we need to distribute the 5 out of the binomial like so:

$$\frac{5x + 15}{5} = \frac{5(x + 3)}{5}$$

This problem takes a little vision because you need to find an opportunity to factor out a number that can cancel with the divisor. So the goal in the above example is to factor 5 out of the top equation. This case works fine.

$$\frac{5(x + 3)}{5} = x + 3$$

We can apply the same concept to an even more complicated example. To divide $x^2 + 2xy + 4$ by x, for example, factor out x from the top equation, like so:

$$\frac{x^2 + 2xy + 4}{x} = \frac{x(x + 2y + \frac{4}{x})}{x}$$

Well, the 4 didn't factor very smoothly, but we did manage to factor x out of the denominator, giving us the final answer of:

$$\frac{x(x + 2y + \frac{4}{x})}{x} = x + 2y + \frac{4}{x}$$

This is as difficult as polynomial problems get. We'll provide you with a few practice examples at the end of the chapter drill.

Binomials and Trinomials

Factoring binomials and trinomials will be no problem if you followed the steps above describing how to multiply and divide polynomials. Factoring is the process by which we remove the greatest common factor in order to rewrite the expression in a simpler expression. Let's start with the building block of polynomials—the binomial expression—and use the relatively simple expression: $x^2 + x$. What algebraic factor do both terms in the binomial have in common? It's easy to see that x is common to both x^2 and x. Since we have a common term, this expression can be rewritten by factoring x out of the equation like so:

$$x^2 + x = x(x + 1)$$

Remember: GCF stands for the Greatest Common Factor. The GCF of $6xy + 3x$ is $3x$, because $3x$ is the largest monomial that can be divided evenly into the polynomial, $6xy + 3x$.

The goal is always to find the greatest common factor (GCF)—x in the above example. When we factor out our GCF, all addition and subtraction should take place within parentheses. This is the case with the example above. The GCF is not limited to one-variable expressions, so we need to be able to find a GCF with multiple variables taken to varying degrees of exponents. For example, the equation $2x^2y + xy$ has like terms in both x and y, as both elements in the binomial contains these two variables. Only the first term has x squared, so we can only factor a single xy out of the equation, as we have done below:

$$2x^2y + xy = xy(2x + 1)$$

We've completed our two goals with factoring. We found our GCF (xy) and successfully placed all addition and subtraction into parentheses, $(2x + 1)$.

Common FOIL Identities

Factoring can get a little complicated, so there are a few FOIL identities that can help you handle the more complex factoring on the exam. Certain "factoring patterns" can reduce large expressions to their simplest form. We're going to cover the three major identities that will help you solve the more complicated factoring problems quickly and efficiently. We'll also show you why Plugging In may become your all-time favorite factoring tool.

Differences of Squares

$$x^2 - y^2 = (x + y)(x - y)$$

This is an important identity to memorize. If we FOIL $(x + y)(x - y)$, it will turn into $x^2 - y^2$. It would be a great exercise for you to take a moment to verify this on paper. Your goal is to memorize this identity and know it backward and forward. In order to identify the differences between two squares as equal to $(x + y)(x - y)$, you will need to understand this equality in reverse. Here's an example so you can see why this is important:

$$\frac{z^2 - y^2}{z - y}$$

At first glance, this question would seem to be in its most simple form. That's why memorizing the differences between two squares is so important. If we convert $z^2 - y^2$ into its equivalent $(z + y)(z - y)$, we can see how important this equality really is.

$$\frac{z^2 - y^2}{z - y} = \frac{(z + y)(z - y)}{z - y}$$

What can we do next? If you said cross out the $(z - y)$ on both the top and bottom, you're right on the money.

$$\frac{(z + y)(z - y)}{z - y} = z + y$$

So, an expression that initially looked unsolvable actually reduces to a relatively simple $(z + y)$. That's why memorizing the difference of squares is crucially important in factoring. $z^2 - y^2$ is equal to $(z + y)(z - y)$.

> $(x + y)(x - y)$ are called conjugate pairs. When you multiply conjugate pairs, you get the difference of two perfect squares: $x^2 - y^2$

Perfect Square Trinomials

$$(x+y)(x+y) = x^2 + 2xy + y^2$$

Perfect square trinomials are algebraic expressions that will factor out into identical binomials, as illustrated above. You'll notice that this equation follows FOIL exactly; you may want to confirm this on paper. But just like the Difference of Squares formula, it is important to know this identity backward and forward—recognizing that any algebraic expression in the form of $x^2 + 2xy + y^2$ is immediately reducible to $(x+y)(x+y)$. A typical question on the EOC exam could look like this:

Example 1

What is the value of the equation $x^2 + 2xy + y^2$, if x is equal to 38 and y is equal to 62?

A   100

B   1,000

C   10,000

D   100,000

Even using a calculator, there is the potential for careless mistakes on this problem. The student who recognizes this equation as a perfect square trinomial avoids that possibility and is rewarded with extra time, because the equation can be easily simplified:

$$x^2 + 2xy + y^2 = (x+y)(x+y) = (62+38)(62+38) = (100)(100) = 10,000$$

This gets us the correct answer of **C**, quickly and painlessly.

There's one other form that a perfect square trinomial could take: The same form as the formula above, except that the perfect squares will be subtracted from one another rather than added.

$$(x-y)(x-y) = x^2 - 2xy + y^2$$

Once again, this follows FOIL, and once again it will be important for you to recognize this both ways.

Trinomials with Binomial Factors or Reverse FOIL

Not all trinomial expressions have perfect squares for their roots, and it's important to know how to apply FOIL in reverse to break down a trinomial into two binomial factors, when possible. Running FOIL in reverse requires a touch of mental mathematics (doing the math in your head), but it becomes easier to visualize these problems with practice. Let's run through an example to see if this process is familiar.

$$x^2 + 4x - 21$$

If this trinomial breaks down into two binomials, we know the first terms of each binomial must be x, since the first term in the trinomial is x^2. So, we can quickly rewrite the equation as:

$$(x\_\_)(x\_\_)$$

Now we know from our work with FOIL that the last term is arrived at by multiplying the last two terms together; since this number is negative (-21), we also know that one of these terms is positive and one is negative. Our essential question is this: *What two numbers multiply together to give us −21 and add together to give us +4?* This is where our mental mathematics comes in. Considering the factors of 21, which are 1, 21, 3 and 7, can you think of any way to combine them to arrive at −21 through multiplication and +4 through addition? Hopefully, 7 and 3 come to mind, and now all we need to do is decide which is positive and which is negative. In order to get a +4, we need the 7 positive and the 3 negative. The equation should look like this:

$$x^2 + 4x - 21$$
$$(x - 3)(x + 7)$$

This solution is confirmed using FOIL (which would be a great exercise to do).

Factoring by Grouping

You can't expect the test-writers to give you algebraic terms in the most convenient or recognizable order—making recognition of the FOIL identities that much more important. Let's look at a horrible, nasty algebraic expression:

$$z^2 + x^2 - v^2 + y^2 + 2xy$$

It's probably safe to say that after your initial feeling of revulsion, you might come to the conclusion that this expression cannot be factored, as there are no common factors. This is where grouping comes into play. At a second glance, can you recognize any parts of some familiar FOIL identities? Try rewriting the expression, placing all the x and y terms on the left and the z and v terms on the right. Hopefully, we'll identify some familiar expressions:

$$x^2 + 2xy + y^2 + z^2 - v^2$$

Ah, yes, the difference of 2 squares and a perfect square trinomial are in one equation. We'll add parentheses to help you along. We can rewrite $x^2 + 2xy + y^2$ as $(x + y)(x + y)$, and rewrite $z^2 - v^2$ as $(z + v)(z - v)$, giving us a simplified expression of:

$$(x + y)(x + y) + (z + v)(z - v)$$

That's it; it's simplified. Confused? If so, don't worry. We're about to show you how to turn some factoring questions into simple arithmetic questions—remember Plugging In?

Plugging In on Factoring Questions

Here is a complicated factoring problem that will horrify you, then delight you. Observe:

Example 2

Which of the following is the factored version of this given algebraic expression: $2(x^2 + 2xy + y^2)$?

F $2(x + y)^2$

G $(x + y)^3$

H $2x + 2y + 4$

J $2x^2 + 2y^2$

Wouldn't this be fun to factor? Let's not. Let's Plug In and say $x = 2$, and $y = 3$ (simple, easy integers), and see what that expression in the question gives us:

$$2\left((2)^2 + 2(2)(3) + (3)^2\right) = 2(4 + 12 + 9) = 2(25) = 50$$

So, when x is 2 and y is 3, the equation equals 50—our **target**. Only one answer choice should give us 50 when we plug these numbers into our answer choices. Let's try it out:

F $\quad 2(2+3)^2 = 50$ (*yeah!*)

G $\quad (2+3)^3 = 125$ (*boooob*)

H $\quad 2(2) + 2(3) + 4 = 14$ (*nope*)

J $\quad 2(2)^2 + 2(3)^2 = 22$ (*nub–ub*)

That couldn't be easier. Factoring will also work, and sometimes the test will design problems that resist Plugging In and force you to factor to get the right answer. But when you are given an algebraic problem with variables in the answer choice, Plugging In can make a huge difference in your score. Plugging In is faster and allows you to work and double check a problem at the same time. The ability to spot and execute Plug In questions is critical, and you should keep this in the back of your mind as you work the following drill:

Factoring Drill

1   **Simplify the following expression:** $4x^2y + (xy + 7) + x^2y + (2xy - 5)$

A $\quad 5x^2 + x^2y^2 - 35$

B $\quad 5x^2y + 2xy - 2$

C $\quad 4x^2(xy) - 2x^2y(xy)$

D $\quad 5x^2y + 3xy + 2$

Here's how to crack it:

Group and combine the like terms. Plugging In is an option, but this is one of the few times when performing the algebra is more efficient. The solution is **D**.

2   If $s = \{4x + 3y - 8\}$, and $n = \{-4y + x + 7\}$, what is the value of $s + n$?

F $3xy - 1$

G $-16xy + 3xy - 56$

H $5x - y - 1$

J $3yx + 1$

Here's how to crack it:

Plugging In would work, but it's better to train yourself to recognize the like terms. The answer is **H**.

3   Which of the following is equivalent to $\dfrac{7x + 28}{14}$?

A $\dfrac{1}{2}x^2 + 2x$

B $7x + 2$

C $\dfrac{x + 4}{2}$

D $\dfrac{x + 2}{7}$

Here's how to crack it:

Remember, you can't divide with nonfactored addition in the numerator. So, you have two options. You could factor out 7 from the top equation by using the reverse distributive property like so:

$$\frac{7x + 28}{14} = \frac{7(x + 4)}{14} = \frac{x + 4}{2}$$

Or, if you were hesitant to factor, Plug In! Only **C** will give you your target.

4 Simplify the following expression: $\dfrac{x^2 - y^2}{x^2 + 2xy + y^2}$

F $\dfrac{1}{2xy}$

G $\dfrac{x-y}{x+y}$

H $\dfrac{x+y}{x-y}$

J   1

Here's how to crack it:

Plug In. Algebraically, this equation represents the difference of two squares divided by a perfect square trinomial, or $\dfrac{(x+y)(x-y)}{(x+y)(x+y)} = \dfrac{x-y}{x+y}$. If this was not immediately apparent, you could simply Plug In a couple of easy integers for x

and y. Only **G** would work out correctly.

5 What is the value of $\dfrac{2x^2 - 1}{2x - 1}$ if $x = -3$?

A -3

B $-\dfrac{17}{7}$

C   3

D   6

Here's how to crack it:

Plug In the number and solve. If $x = -3$, $\dfrac{2x^2 - 1}{2x - 1}$ reduces to $\dfrac{2(-3)^2 - 1}{2(-3) - 1} = \dfrac{2(9) - 1}{-6 - 1} = \dfrac{17}{-7}$.

This should have been easy. The correct answer is **B**.

6   **What is the value of** $\dfrac{2x^2 y + xy + 15y}{2x^2 + x + 15}$ **if** $x = 17$ **and** $y = -30$?

     F -510

     G -30

     H 30

     J 510

Here's how to crack it:

Now we're having fun. Plugging In is certainly an option, but there's no doubt that the test-taker who recognizes the following factoring pattern will have a quick and easy time with this question: $\dfrac{y(2x^2 + x + 15)}{2x^2 + x + 15} = y = -30$, or **G**. We're just trying to keep you on your toes. There are usually multiple ways to solve a problem on a standardized test, and some can be faster than others. Plugging In would have resulted in some messy calculations, and in this case, the factoring was quicker.

7 Factor completely: $x^2 - 2x - 63$

    A $(x - 7)(x - 9)$

    B $(x + 7)(x - 9)$

    C $(x - 7)(x + 9)$

    D $(x + 7)(x + 9)$

Here's how to crack it:

Use reverse FOIL or Plugging In using FOIL—it's up to you. The correct answer is **B**.

8 Which of the following represents $\dfrac{x^2 + 16x + 64}{x^2 + 3x - 40}$ in its completely factored form?

    F $x + 8$

    G $x - 5$

    H $\dfrac{x + 8}{x - 5}$

    J $\dfrac{x - 5}{x + 8}$

Here's how to crack it:

Again, you can Plug In or factor. This might be easy enough to just

Plug In for x. If you did, and used 2 for x, the equation would be rewritten like this:

$\dfrac{4 + 32 + 64}{4 + 6 - 40} = \dfrac{100}{-30} = \dfrac{-10}{3}$. You'd quickly find that only **H** gives you the same answer when

using $x = 2$.

> *Remember:* When in doubt on a factoring question, PLUG IN!

Chapter 5

The Equation and the Graph

Contrary to popular belief, algebra was not invented to torture millions of unsuspecting teenagers. Algebra is a way of describing how mathematical relationships look on a coordinate plane (or Cartesian grid). The equations that we reviewed in the last chapter were referred to as linear because, when graphed, they make a straight line. There are various ways that linear equations can be turned into graphs, however, and you can bet that your Algebra I EOC exam will test you on all of them.

In this chapter we're going to discuss the relationship between algebraic equations and their graph. It might not be a bad idea to have some graph paper handy, just in case you'd like to double-check some of your work.

The Coordinate Plane (or Cartesian Grid)

The coordinate plane is the grid on which an equation's points are located. Algebra can be very confusing if you don't realize the visual (graphing) descriptions that each equation generates—and this exam seems particularly concerned with how equations generate graphs.

Ordered Pairs

The first thing to know about the coordinate plane is that its points are called **ordered pairs.** An ordered pair is two numbers that describe a single point on the coordinate plane. An ordered pair will always be in the form of (x, y), where x runs horizontally and y runs vertically. Take for example the ordered pair $(2, 8)$, and recall how we would plot this point on a coordinate plane.

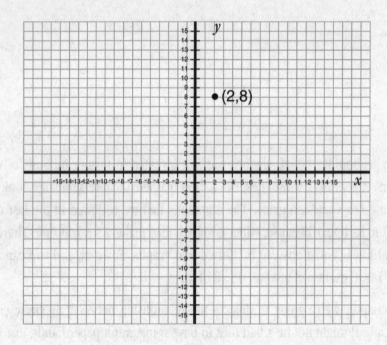

Starting with the x-coordinate, +2, we start at the **origin** (point O, O) and move 2 spaces to the right on the x-axis. We then move +8 on the y-axis. If we took another ordered pair, (−2, −4), and plotted it on the same grid, we could draw a line through the two points like so:

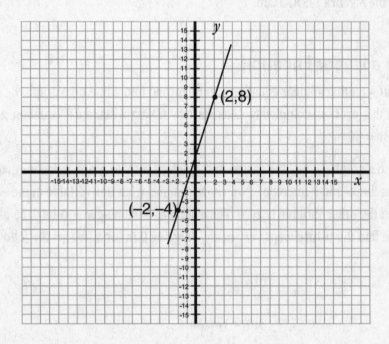

Another way this line can be represented is through an equation. In this case:

$$y = 3x + 2$$

The points described above fit into this equation—a fact we can check by plugging in the ordered pairs listed above back into the equation. Let's try the second point (−4, −2), just to be sure.

$$(-4) = 3(-2) + 2$$
$$(-4) = -6 + 2$$
$$(-4) = -4$$

> **Remember:** The ordered pair is always x before y. To help you remember, think of the rhyme: x before y, walk before you fly.

Yep, it fits. As does the ordered pair, (2, 8). Everything in this chapter stems from the simple act of drawing a line between two (or more) points and understanding the relationship of that line to linear equations, such as the one listed above. We'll look at the various ways that linear equations and functions can produce ordered pairs and lines on a graph. This is a central focus of the Algebra I EOC exam.

Graphing With a Linear Equation

There are several ways that a linear equation can be turned into a line on a graph. Be sure you understand this process completely. Let's start by taking a standard equation as an example: $5x + 3y = 30$.

Let's turn this into a graph. One of the easiest and quickest ways to graph a linear equation is to "zero in" on the x- and y-intercepts, which determines what one variable in the equation equals when the other variable is zero. For example, if we plug $x = 0$ into the above equation, we can find the **y-intercept** very easily. Plugging 0 in for x, we get the following results:

$$5(0) + 3y = 30$$
$$3y = 30$$
$$\frac{3}{3}y = \frac{30}{3}$$
$$y = 10$$

So, when the x-coordinate is at 0, we know that y is at 10, producing an ordered pair (0, 10) that can be represented on the graph—indicating the **y-intercept** of this equation. We now know that our line will cross the y-axis at 10. To get our second ordered pair and complete our line, we must find out what x equals when $y = 0$:

$$5x + 3(0) = 30$$
$$5x = 30$$
$$\frac{5}{5}x = \frac{30}{5}$$
$$x = 6$$

We've found that when $y = 0$, then $x = 6$, giving us the second ordered pair we need to make the line, $(6, 0)$. This is the **x-intercept**, or the point on the x-axis where the line passes through, leaving us with the following graph:

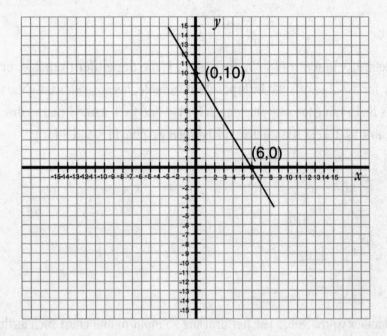

All right! We got our line by means of the x- and y-intercepts, and we've also begun to explore the fundamental way linear equations produce ordered pairs. Let's look at another way to the test may ask us to recognize the equation of specific line.

Plug $x = 0$ into an equation to find its *y-intercept*; plug $y = 0$ to find its *x-intercept*.

Graphing With a Linear Function

Linear equations and functions are almost the same thing, except they are expressed differently. A linear function is expressed in variables, such as x and y. For example, if we take a normal linear equation, $2x - y = 7$, we could easily rewrite this equation as a linear function—having one variable depend upon the value of the other. Let's rewrite this equation as a function so that x depends on y:

$$2x - y = 7$$

$$2x = 7 + y$$

$$\frac{2}{2}x = \frac{7+y}{2}$$

$$x = \frac{7+y}{2}$$

We've now defined x in terms of y. In this case, x is the **dependent** variable, because it depends on y for its value. y is the **independent** variable, because it dictates the value we get for x. Let's find a value for x by plugging in for y—and we'll make y odd so that the sum is evenly divisible by 2. Let's see what x equals when we plug in 3 and 5 for y:

$$x = \frac{7+(3)}{2} \qquad\qquad x = \frac{7+(5)}{2}$$

$$x = \frac{10}{2} \qquad\qquad\qquad x = \frac{12}{2}$$

$$x = 5 \qquad\qquad\qquad\qquad x = 6$$

You may remember your algebra teacher drawing an input-output chart such as this:

X	Y
5	3
6	5

> A linear function is an expression in which one variable is defined in terms of another variable, such as $y = 3x + 2$.

There are several ways to get enough ordered pairs to make a graph. In order to simplify the many different options in writing linear equations, there is an accepted **General Equation of a Line**, in which the key concept of **Slope** is incorporated.

The Slope

The slope is the visual representation of an equation's rate of change on a graph. It is a primary topic that you'll be tested on in the Algebra I exam, so make sure you understand it fully. Let's review how we find a slope and then learn to crack this type of question.

There are two important formulas that apply to slope. Memorize both of them.

$$y = mx + b$$

This is the equation of a line, where *y* represents the *y*-coordinate, *x* represents the *x*-coordinate, *b* represents the *y*-intercept, and *m* represents the slope. To make things even more fun, the slope of the line (*m*) has its own formula that looks like this:

$$Slope = \frac{Rise\,(change\,in\,y)}{Run\,(change\,in\,x)}$$

This means that when a linear equation (an equation with no exponents or square roots) is graphed, the result will be a straight line that shows the line's rate of change. Let's look at the four possible outcomes when a linear equation is graphed and see what they tell us about the rate of change of the line. We'll look at a **positive slope**, a **negative slope**, a **slope of zero,** and an **undefined slope**.

> **Remember:** It is absolutely essential that you memorize the equation of a line: $y = mx + b$. *y* represents the *y*-coordinate, *x* represents the *x*-coordinate, *b* represents the *y*-intercept, and *m* represents the slope.

Take the points (2, 5) and (3, 8) and plot them on a plane as we've done below:

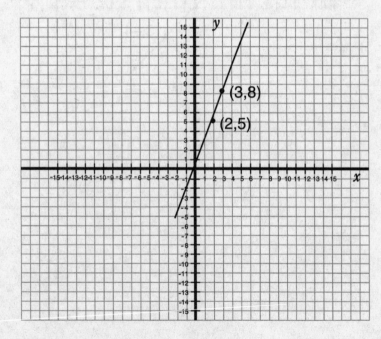

Remember: You *must* memorize the equation of a slope:

$$Slope = \frac{Rise\,(change\,in\,y)}{Run\,(change\,in\,x)}$$

Note that as the graph moves from left to right, the line goes up, indicating a positive slope. A positive slope means that the *y*-coordinate gets larger as the *x*-coordinate moves to the right. When we plug into the slope formula with our two original points, this result is verified like so:

$$\frac{change\,in\,y}{change\,in\,x} = \frac{8-5}{3-2} = \frac{3}{1} = 3$$

Remember: When determining the changes in *x* and *y*, it doesn't matter which ordered pair you start with, as long as you're consistent in your application. If we started with (2, 5), we would get negative values for both *y* and *x*, which still reduces to positive 3. So, as we've seen above, a positive slope represents an increasing *y* for an increasing *x*. With this example we found that for every unit that *x* increases on the graph, *y* will increase by 3. Now let's take another set of points (−3, 2) and (3, −4) and see how it differs.

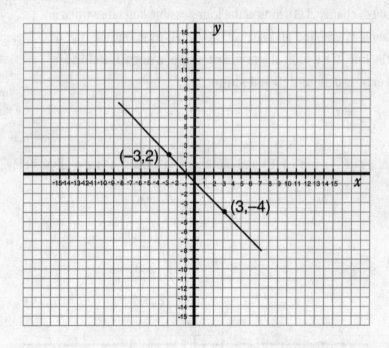

Notice now that y decreases as x increases, causing the line to descend as it goes from left to right. This is a negative slope. And, as expected, we get a negative result when we plug these coordinates into the slope formula:

$$\frac{rise\,(change\ in\ y)}{run\,(change\ in\ x)} = \frac{-4-2}{3--3} = \frac{-6}{6} = -1$$

So, a slope of −1 simply means that as x increases by 1, y will decrease by 1. In our graph above, the line intercepts the y-axis at −1. Let's plug one of our ordered pairs (−3, 2) into the equation, and using our slope of −1, see if the value for b (the y-intercept) gives us the −1 value we got on our graph:

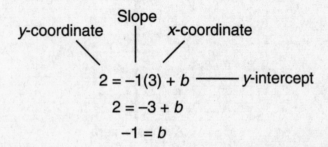

Bingo! Both the graph and the equation gave us −1. Now we know we're on the right track. Notice the similarities between the equation and the graph. They are describing the same concept in different ways—one visually, one mathematically. The EOC exam in Algebra I will test both types of expressions.

An Undefined or Zero Slope

Besides being positive or negative, two other possibilities can arise when graphing linear equations on a graph: a **slope of zero** and an **undefined slope**. They could show up on your test, so let's review.

> **Remember:** Any attempt to divide by 0 results in an undefined solution.

A slope of zero represents an equation in which y does not change at all as x increases. When graphed, an equation with a slope of zero will yield a straight horizontal line running parallel to the x-axis:

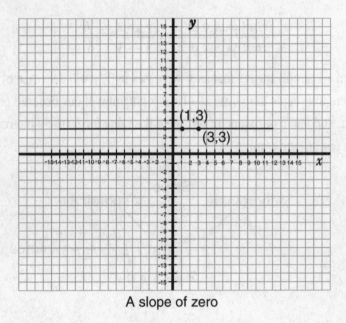

A slope of zero

Notice that when we plot the points $(1, 3)$ and $(3, 3)$, they yield a straight line when graphed. Also notice that when we plug into the slope formula, the y-coordinates cancel each other out, yielding a value of zero.

$$\frac{Rise(change\ in\ y)}{Run(change\ in\ x)} = \frac{3-3}{3-1} = \frac{0}{2} = 0$$

The test may also present an **undefined slope**, a slope in which the x-coordinates cancel one another out, yielding a line that runs parallel to the y-axis. This is tricky, because although the slope cannot be determined, the relationship can still be represented on a graph, as we've done below with the points $(3, 4)$, and $(3, -3)$:

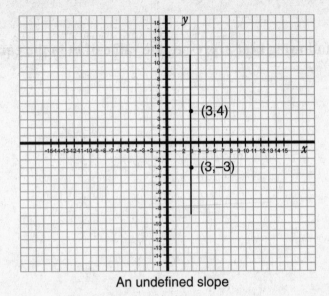
An undefined slope

When we graph the points $(3, 4)$ and $(3, -3)$, the result is a straight vertical line parallel to the y-axis. A slope defines the change in y as x increases, but in this case, x does not increase at all. So by definition, there can be no slope. And, not surprisingly, when we plug these coordinates into the slope formula, we get an undefined slope.

A slope of 0 is a horizontal line on a graph. An undefined slope is a vertical line.

$$\frac{Rise(change\ in\ y)}{Run(change\ in\ x)} = \frac{-3-4}{3-3} = \frac{-7}{0} = Undefined$$

Now that we've reviewed the slope of a linear equation, let's look at a few sample questions that could show up on your exam. Don't forget that when given its equation, you will be asked to determine the slope of a line. This type of question will break down into algebraic manipulation. However, you could always use your graphing calculator to check your solution. The EOC exam will also ask you to deduce the slope from a given graph of a line. After our work above, this will be a breeze. Let's try a few drills.

Example 1

Which of the following best expresses the value of *m* in the equation
$10 = 3m + 4$?

A $-\dfrac{2}{1}$

B $\dfrac{2}{1}$

C $\dfrac{1}{2}$

D $-\dfrac{1}{2}$

Here's how to crack it:

This question breaks down into pure algebra. $6 = 3m$, so *m* should be solved to be 2, making **B** the correct choice.

Example 2

What is the slope of the line in the graph below?

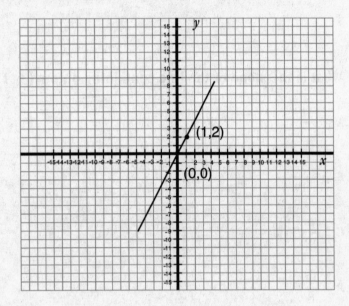

F $\frac{2}{1}$

G $\frac{1}{2}$

H $-\frac{1}{2}$

J $-\frac{2}{1}$

Here's how to crack it:

There are several ways to approach this question. First, let's use the process of elimination (POE). Since y is increasing as x moves from left to right, the slope must be positive—so **H** and **J** can be eliminated. From there, you can just look at the graph and notice that as x moves to the right one unit, y has clearly jumped more than $\frac{1}{2}$. So the only remaining choice is **F**. You could also find two points on the line and compute the answer with the slope formula. Let's try it to be sure.

> **Remember:** When using the slope formula, it makes no difference what ordered pair you start with—as long as you're consistent.

$$\frac{Rise(change\ in\ y)}{Run(change\ in\ x)} = \frac{2-0}{1-0} = \frac{2}{1} = 2$$

Example 3

What is the slope of the line containing points (3, 12) and (−3, −7)?

A $\quad -\dfrac{19}{6}$

B $\quad -\dfrac{6}{19}$

C $\quad \dfrac{6}{19}$

D $\quad \dfrac{19}{6}$

Here's how to crack it:

Just plug the points into the formula! You should get **D**.

$$\frac{-7-12}{-3-3} = \frac{-19}{-6} = \frac{19}{6} = \frac{Rise}{Run}$$

Finding Equations

The skills we've reviewed so far in this chapter are all related to the general equation of a line. We've learned how to calculate slopes and points from equations, but now we have to work backward—calculating equations from points and slopes. If you are comfortable with everything so far, this should be a cinch.

Finding the Equation of a Line From the Slope

When given the graph of a linear equation, the key to finding the equation is to focus in on the y-intercept and plug its value into the general equation of a line $(y = mx + b)$. Then calculate the slope from points on the line to get the actual equation. Let's try a quick example. Say we want to know the equation of the following graph:

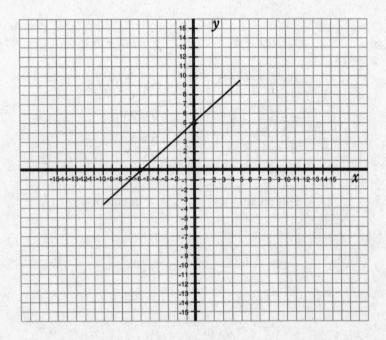

What do we know from looking at this graph? Certainly the y-intercept, as the line is clearly intercepting the y-axis at +5. Let's incorporate this into our general equation of a line as $y = mx + 5$. To finish the job, we need to find the slope—by zeroing in on the x- and y-intercepts. Referring to the above graph, we already know that the y-intercept is at point (0, 5). Since the line crosses the x-axis at –6, another point on this graph is (–6, 0). Recall the slope formula and we'll get our equation of a line.

$$(0,5)\,and\,(-6,0)$$

$$m = \frac{y_2 - y_2}{x_2 - x_1}$$

$$\frac{rise}{run} = \frac{0-5}{-6-0} = \frac{-5}{-6} = \frac{5}{6}$$

$$slope = \frac{5}{6}$$

Remember: This is not the only way to find the equation of a line from a graph, but it's the easiest. Let's look at another way they ask us to form the equation of a line.

You can tell we're on the right track because our slope is positive and our graph increases from left to right. To find the equation of this line, let's add our slope value to the equation, giving us $y = \frac{5}{6}x + 5$. Note that both our x- and y-intercepts plug into this equation perfectly, confirming our answer:

$$y = mx + b$$
$$0 = \frac{5}{6}(-6) + 5$$
$$0 = \frac{-30}{6} + 5$$
$$0 = -5 + 5$$
$$0 = 0$$

y-intercept

$$y = mx + b$$
$$5 = \frac{5}{6}(0) + 5$$
$$5 = 0 + 5$$
$$5 = 5$$

x-intercept

Finding the Equation of a Line From Two Points On the Line

The key to finding an equation of a line by using only two of its points will still be the slope—but now the y-intercept will be harder to find because we may not have a graph to look at. With two points of a line we can easily compute its slope—which should be second nature before you take the Algebra I EOC exam. After we obtain our slope, we'll plug the slope into the equation of a line and solve for our y-intercept. Say that we wanted to write the equation of a line that passes through $(3, -6)$ and $(-2, 4)$: With the points $(3, -6)$ the 3 is x_1, and the -6 is y_1. For the second coordinate points, -2 is x_2 and 4 is y_2.

$$\frac{4 - (-6)}{-2 - 3} = \frac{10}{-5} = -2 (slope)$$

Let's put this slope back into the linear equation: $y = -2x + b$. We find that our only unknown variable is b (or the y-intercept), which we can solve with the slope of a line and any known point on it. We'll plug in our slope and the first point from the line $(-2, 4)$.

$$y = mx + b$$
$$y = -2x + b$$
$$4 = -2(-2) + b$$
$$4 = 4 + b$$
$$0 = b$$

So the y-intercept is 0, which we can quickly confirm by plugging in the other point on our line.

$$y = mx + b$$
$$y = -2x + b$$
$$-6 = -2(3) + b$$
$$-6 = -6 + b$$
$$0 = b$$

With our solution confirmed, we can formulate the equation of this line as

$$y = -2x + 0, \text{ or } y = -2x.$$

Finding the Equation of a Line With a Slope and One Point on a Line

This is the easiest way to find the equation of line. Simply plug in your point and slope to the general equation of a line and solve for your y-intercept. For example, if you know that a line contains a point of $(-6, 4)$ and has a slope of $\frac{3}{2}$, the y-intercept is only moments away.

$$y = mx + b$$
$$4 = \frac{3}{2}(-6) + b$$
$$4 = -9 + b$$
$$13 = b$$

The equation of a line is $y = mx + b$, where m is the slope and b is the y-intercept. This is *very* important! Knowing this formula could make the difference in passing the exam.

So our y intercept is 13, and we can now write the equation of this line as $y = \frac{3}{2}x + 13$, indicating a positive slope.

Slopes and Equations Drills

We hope that our review of slopes and graphing has been helpful, but make sure to clear up any confusion you may have with your algebra teacher. The Algebra I EOC exam will expect you to know the relationship between a linear equation and its graph backward and forward. To help you, we've written a few practice problems that will ensure that you're clear on these important concepts.

1   **Which of the following is the graph of a line with a *y*-intercept of −4 and a slope of −4?**

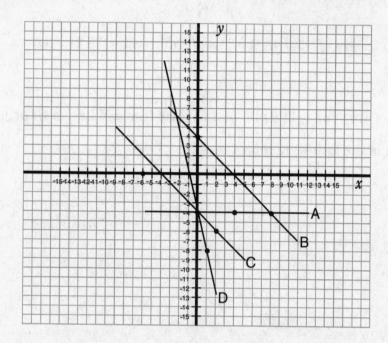

Here's how to crack it:

As with most slope questions, there are a variety of ways to knock this problem out. We should eliminate **B,** because it doesn't have a *y*-intercept of −4. We know the slope is not 0, which is what **A** (or any other horizontal line) is. ***Remember:*** A slope of −4 means that as *x* increases one unit, *y* should decrease by 4—and you can see that only **D** drops 4 units as *x* increases by 1. Solving with the equation of a line might be a bit too much work.

2   **Which of the following ordered pairs would be produced by the equation**

$$-3x + y = 11?$$

    F   (−3, 2) and (0, 11)

    G   (2, −3) and (0, 11)

    H   (−3, 2) and (11, 0)

    J   (2, −3) and (11, 0)

111

Here's how to crack it:

Backsolve, all day and all night. Only **F** provides both points that correctly complete the equation.

$$-3(-3) + 2 = 9 + 2 = 11 \ and -3(0) + 11 = 0 + 11 = 11$$

3 Points $(x, 4)$ and $(-3, 9)$ lie on the same line and have a slope of $\frac{1}{3}$. Which of the following represents x?

A   −18

B   −12

C   12

D   18

Here's how to crack it:

Remember the slope formula: $m = \dfrac{y_2 - y_1}{x_2 - x_1}$

$$\frac{1}{3} = \frac{9-4}{-3-x}$$
$$\frac{5}{-3-x} = \frac{1}{3} =$$
$$-3-x = 15$$
$$\underline{+3 \qquad +3}$$
$$-x = 18$$
$$\frac{-x}{-1} = \frac{18}{-1}$$
$$x = -18$$

The correct answer is **A**.

4 What is the equation of the following line?

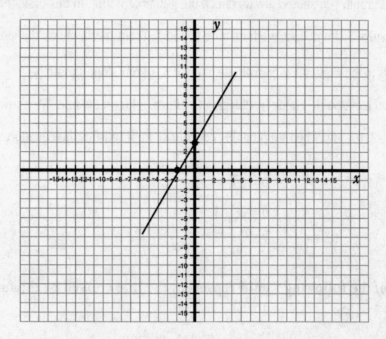

F $y = \dfrac{2}{3}x + 3$

G $y = \dfrac{2}{3}x - 3$

H $y = \dfrac{3}{2}x + 3$

J $y = \dfrac{3}{2}x - 3$

Here's how to crack it:

From a visual graph, you should always check the *y*-intercept first. In this case, the *y*-intercept is at positive 3, immediately eliminating **G** and **J**. From there, check the slope; as *x* moved 2 units to the right, the *y*-coordinate jumped 3, so our slope should be $+\frac{3}{2}$, leaving us with **H**. You can double-check by Plugging In either point on the line. We know one coordinate (−2, 0), and when we plug this coordinate in, it satisfies the equation.

$$0 = \frac{3}{2}(-2) + 3$$
$$0 = -3 + 3$$
$$0 = 0$$

5 **Which of the following would represent the line created by the function *y* = 2*x* − 5?**

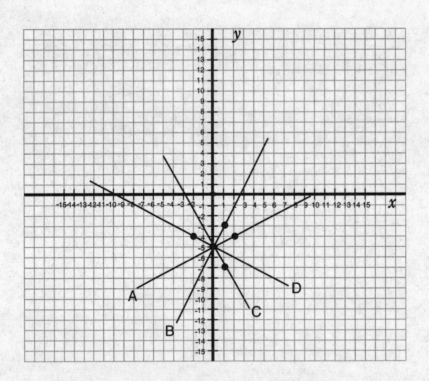

Here's how to crack it:

The *y*-intercept doesn't help us here (they're all –5), so let's hit the slope right away. The equation should have a positive slope of 2, which means that **C** and **D** are eliminated. From there, we can just eyeball which line moves up 2 when *x* increases by 1. That would be **B**.

> **Remember.** A positive slope will move upward when moving from left to right, a negative slope downward.

6   What is the slope of the following graph?

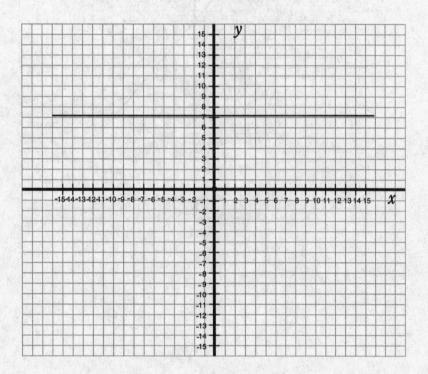

F   Undefined

G   0

H   1

J   Infinite

Here's how to crack it:

A flat line is a slope of 0 (*y* not increasing with *x*), and a vertical line is a slope of undefined. So the answer is **G**.

7 What is the slope of the line in the following graph?

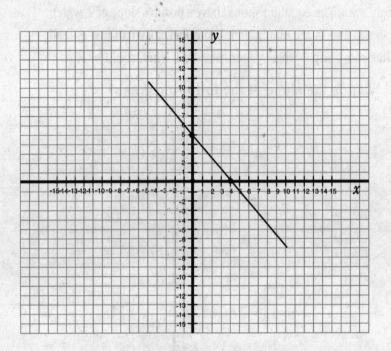

A $-\dfrac{5}{4}$

B $-\dfrac{4}{5}$

C $\dfrac{4}{5}$

D $\dfrac{5}{4}$

Here's how to crack it:

The line tilts down, so the slope must be negative. Closer inspection yields a change of -5 in

y as x moves 4 to the right, giving us a rise/run of $-\dfrac{5}{4}$, or **A**.

8 What is the x-intercept of a line that has a y-intercept of -2 and a slope of 3?

F $\quad -\dfrac{2}{3}$

G $\quad -\dfrac{1}{6}$

H $\quad \dfrac{1}{6}$

J $\quad \dfrac{2}{3}$

Here's how to crack it:

y will equal 0 at the x-intercept, so let's take what information we have and plug it into the equation of a line. From $0 = 3(x) - 2$, we find that x will equal $\dfrac{2}{3}$ when y is 0, so the x-intercept must be $\dfrac{2}{3}$, or **J**.

9 What is the equation of a line that contains points $(-3, 5)$ and $(7, 12)$?

A $\quad y = \dfrac{10}{7}x + 7.1$

B $\quad y = \dfrac{10}{7}x - 7.1$

C $\quad y = \dfrac{7}{10}x + 7.1$

D $\quad y = \dfrac{7}{10}x - 7.1$

Here's how to crack it:

Once again, the equation of a slope (m) is $\dfrac{y_2 - y_1}{x_2 - x_1}$. Then, once you've got the slope (m),

plug into the equation of a line which is $y = mx + b$. Plug in the points to each of the

formulas. Both points must plug successfully into the right answer. You could also quickly

solve for the slope with a rise/run of $\dfrac{12-5}{7--3} = \dfrac{7}{10}$, and this will eliminate **A** and **B**, which

have the slopes reversed. Both points plug in successfully with

C: $5 = \dfrac{7}{10}(-3) + 7.1$ and $12 = \dfrac{7}{10}(7) + 7.1$

10 **Which of the following would be the graph of $y = 2x - 4$ if the slope were doubled?**

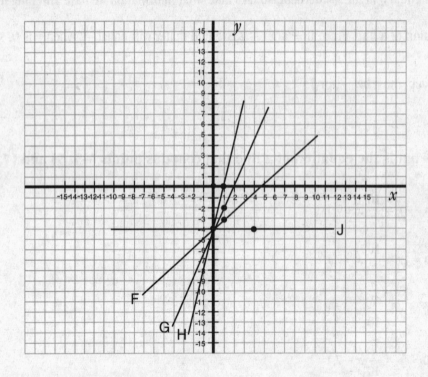

Here's how to crack it:

The slope in the given equation is 2, meaning if it were doubled you'd have a slope of 4. **J** is

wrong because it has a slope of 0, and only **H** jumps up 4 as x moves 1 to the right.

Graphing Multiple Linear Equations

We have established that any linear equation (an equation without exponents or square roots) will make a line on a coordinate plane. So, if you have two linear equations that create lines on the same coordinate plane, these two lines usually intersect. Systems of equations describe the point in which these two lines intersect (or not in a few cases), and we have to be familiar with the various ways to solve for the point of intersection.

Let's look at a standard graph of two equations to better understand what we need to do. Take two linear equations that will be graphed on the same coordinate plane:

$$2x + y = 8 \text{ and } 2x + 6y = 18$$

To illustrate why such systems of equations even exist (in case you were snoozing that day in algebra), let's graph these lines and note the point of intersection—by finding the x- and y-intercepts for each line. Plugging in $y = 0$ to the above equations, we find that $2x + y = 8$ has an x-intercept of $(4, 0)$. *Remember:* $y = 0$ at the x-intercept, so we solve as

$$2x + 0 = 8$$
$$2x = 8$$
$$x = 4$$

With our y-intercept of $(0, 8)$, we now have enough to create a line. Remember, at the y-intercept, x must be 0, so $2(0) + y = 8$, or $y = 8$. Our other equation, $2x + 6y = 18$, has an x-intercept of $(9, 0)$ and a y-intercept of $(0, 3)$. We now have 2 points for each equation that we can represent on the graph with a line, which we've done below.

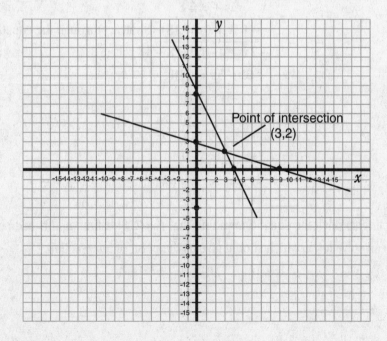

Point of intersection (3,2)

When we graph both lines, we find that they meet at point (3, 2). The whole idea of solving systems of equations is to find the point of intersection—the one point that both linear equations have in common. Fortunately, there are several methods that allow us to find this common point much more quickly than by graphing the equations. You'll need to understand the relationship between the graph and equations, but you won't have to graph every equation to find the solution! Let's look at a very effective way to solve for systems of equations, using the same two equations we used above.

Finding the Common Point of Multiple Linear Equations

Solving a system of equations by elimination is a quick and effective way to solve for the common point of two linear equations. However, it only works when you have a common term in both equations. You just need to add or subtract the two equations to eliminate the common term and solve for the other variable. Let's see how this works:

$$2x + y = 8$$
$$2x + 6y = 18$$

First, let's identify the common term, in this case $2x$. We want to eliminate the $2x$ from both sides of the equation. Since both are positive, we'll simply subtract the second equation from the first (changing all the signs of the second equation):

$$2x + y = 8$$
$$\underline{- (2x + 6y = 18)} \text{ (Subtract through the equation)}$$
$$2x - 2x + y - 6y = 8 - 18$$
$$0x - 5y = -10$$
$$-5y = -10$$
$$\frac{-5y}{-5} = \frac{-10}{-5}$$
$$y = 2$$

So, by subtracting through the equation, we find that $y = 2$. Substituting this back into the equation, we can solve for x, which should give us the point of intersection.

$$2x + 2 = 8$$
$$\underline{-2 \quad -2}$$
$$\frac{2}{2}x = \frac{6}{2}$$
$$x = 3$$

According to our calculations, these lines intersect at point $(3, 2)$. And if you recall our graph a couple of pages ago, that's exactly what we found. Notice that it also plugs in perfectly to our other equation, as $2(3) + 6(2) = 18$, confirming our solution.

Solving Systems of Equations by Substitution

When you've got two equations that don't have common terms (which can quickly cancel out), you're forced to solve either by substitution or multiplication and elimination. Fortunately for us, this tiresome method is entirely unnecessary on a standardized exam. For example, let's say the test gave you a question that looked something like this:

Example 1

What is the solution to the following system of equations?

$$\begin{cases} 2x - 5y = -10 \\ -6x - y = 26 \end{cases}$$

A $x = 0, y = 2$

B $x = 2, y = -38$

C $x = \dfrac{-35}{8}, y = \dfrac{1}{4}$

D $x = 5, y = 4$

This problem won't work with all of the quicker ways of solving for x and y. However, never sweat the heavy algebra if there are real numbers in the answers listed below the question. We're not even going to show you how to solve this problem by substitution or subtraction because it's completely unnecessary. Simply **Backsolve!**

We know the answer has to be **A**, **B**, **C**, or **D**, so let's start with **A** and **B**, since they have whole numbers. When we make $x = 0$ and $y = 2$, the first equation solves perfectly. But the point will have to solve for both equations, and when we plug in $(0, 2)$ for the second equation, $0 - 2 \neq 26$—so **A** cannot be the right answer. Similarly, answer choice **B** works for the second equation and not the first. Now we're left with **C** and **D**. Now those hard-earned dollars you spent on this book are really going to pay off. Try **D** first, because those numbers are easier to Plug in. The ordered pair solves for the first equation, but doesn't cut it for the second. The answer **must be C**, since it's the only one left—and we don't even have to go through the trouble of plugging those nasty fractions into the equation!

Never underestimate the power of shortcuts. You should never solve any system of equations that have the answers listed below the question. Attack the answers and save yourself a lot of work.

Parallel and Simultaneous Lines

There are two more possibilities regarding linear equations on a graph that you'll need to know in case they come up on the EOC exam. In one case, you could have lines that are parallel to each other, which would never produce a point of intersection. The other case involves two forms of the same linear equation, which would have an infinite number of solutions (i.e., they are the same line). Take the following system of equations:

$$4x - 3y = -12$$
$$12x - 9y = 36$$

Let's zero these equations out and look at them on a graph so we can see what's happening algebraically. The first equation gives us an x-intercept of $(-3, 0)$, and a y-intercept of $(0, 4)$. The other equation provides $(3, 0)$ and $(0, -4)$ for the x and y-intercepts, respectively. Graphed, each line looks like this:

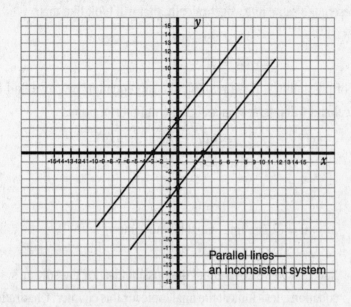

Parallel lines—
an inconsistent system

If we multiply the top equation through by 3, we find an interesting result:

First equation: $4x(3) - 3y(3) = -12(3)$
Second equation: $\underline{12x - 9y = 36}$

or

First equation: $12x - 9y = -36$
Second equation: $\underline{12x - 9y = 36}$

These are virtually the same equations. When we combine the two equations we find that *both* the x and y terms cancel each other out:

$$12x - 9y = -36$$
$$\underline{- (12x - 9y = 36)}$$
$$12x - 12x - 9y + 9y = -36 - 36$$
$$0 = -72?$$

Must be parallel lines

When all of your terms cancel out and there is no solution to the system, the lines must be parallel!

The final possibility is that the exam will give you the exact same equation, meaning that both equations represent the same line. Algebraically, that will look like this:

$$4x + 2y = 10$$
$$8x + 4y = 20$$

This is the simplest of possibilities. If we multiply the top equation by 2, we find that the equations are identical and will intersect in an infinite number of points.

$$4x(2) + 2y(2) = 10(2) = 8x + 2y = 20$$
$$- (8x + 2y) = 20$$

$$0 = 0$$

$0 = 0$? The lines must be the same!

Remember: When all of your terms cancel each other out and there is no solution to the system, the lines must be parallel!

Now that we've covered all the possibilities for the solving systems of equations, let's look at the final topic for this chapter: Quadratic Equations. Then we'll practice some EOC exam material.

Quadratic Equations

Before we learn to solve quadratic equations, let's first learn to identify them. A quadratic equation is any equation in the form $y = ax^2 + bx + c$, though not all of these terms have to be present. All linear equations make straight lines when graphed. Quadratic equations don't make straight lines: They create **parabolas** (big U-shapes). We'll look at three types of quadratic graphs so that we can better understand them.

Graphs of quadratic equations can get complicated, but fortunately for you, they will be relatively easy on the Algebra I EOC exam. It is very unlikely that you'll get any equation that doesn't begin at the origin (0, 0), but we'll show you an example of a quadratic equation that doesn't, just in case. First, let's look at the most elementary of quadratic equations and check out its graph:

$$y = x^2$$

If you remember from the last chapter, we said that any equation without exponents or square roots is called linear, making $y = x^2$ a clear exception. The ordered pairs that this equation produces will be a little different. Since x is squared, y will not be negative for any value that you plug in for x, creating a parabola when graphed. For example, if we plug in 3 for x, we get 9 for y. And conversely, if we plug in -3 for x, we also get 9 for y. Combining these two ordered pairs $(3, 9)$, $(-3, 9)$ with the x- and y-intercepts (conveniently 0 for both in this case), we get a graph that looks like the following:

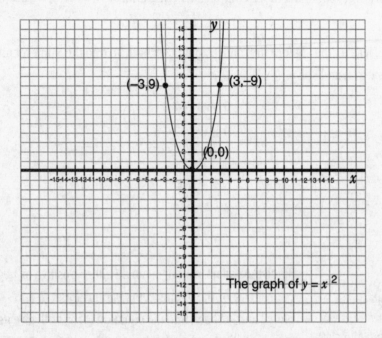

The graph of $y = x^2$

Welcome to the wonderful world of the parabola. If a is greater than 0, the parabola will open upwards. In this case, $a = 1$. Since a is positive in this case, we know that the parabola must open upward. If we graphed $y = -x^2$, then a would equal -1, and we would get the same parabola, except facing down rather than up.

Finding the x-intercept is the primary purpose of solving quadratic equations. In the above example, the parabola crossed the x-axis at exactly one point, the origin $(0, 0)$. In order to find the x-intercept, we set the quadratic equation equal to 0 (what y would be when the x-axis is crossed), and solve. In fact, this is a primary skill that the Algebra I EOC exam will test you on. Take the simple quadratic equation we graphed above. In order to solve it algebraically, we would set y to 0 and solve for x as so:

$$y(0) = x^2$$
$$0 = x^2$$
$$\sqrt{0} = \sqrt{x^2}$$
$$0 = x$$

Our graph on the previous page—which shows that the x-intercept is 0—is confirmed by the algebra. Let's look at a more complicated equation:

$$y = x^2 - 4$$

This time, let's try the algebra first and graphing second. To find the x-intercept(s), we need to set the y to 0 and solve:

$$0 = x^2 - 4$$
$$0 + 4 = x^2 - 4 + 4$$
$$4 = x^2$$
$$\sqrt{4} = \sqrt{x^2}$$
$$2, -2 = x$$

Remember: The square root of a number will have a positive and negative root. In other words, the square root of 4 is not just 2 and −2. This is because both 2 and −2 square to be 4. The SOL test will likely only test you on the positive roots of square roots, however.

Since the square root of 4 can be either positive or negative, the x-coordinate of the x-intercepts should be at 2 and −2. When we plug 2 and −2 back into the equation for x, both give us 0 for y, and we now have 2 ordered pairs, (2, 0), and (−2, 0). Our origin still falls on the y-axis, which we can confirm by zeroing out x and producing the point (0, −4). The graph looks as follows:

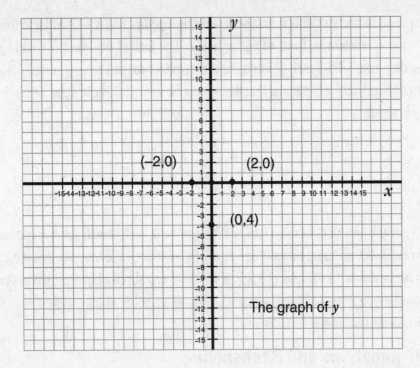

The graph of y

Good. So our solution works out perfectly. When solving quadratic equations, you are simply finding where the parabola crosses the x-axis. Though you want to be able to recognize parabolas like the ones we've drawn above, the EOC exam questions will likely revolve around factoring quadratic equations (when we can't Backsolve the equations).

Factoring Quadratic Equations

Remember FOIL from the last chapter? The key to solving quadratic equations is by throwing this entire process in reverse. For example, let's say we have a quadratic equation in the following form:

$$x^2 - x - 12 = y$$

To find the solution to this equation, we need to set the equation equal to 0 and find where this parabola crosses the x-axis. Then we want to factor this quadratic equation into two **binomials** that can both be set to 0. This sounds complicated, but if you remember FOIL, you'll do fine. Start by adding two parentheses (both starting with x) with which we can isolate our binomials.

$$(x \quad) \quad (x \quad)$$

We then need to know what two numbers multiply together to get -12 and add together to get -1 (the coefficient in front of our x term). The factors of 4 and 3 should pop out because they have a difference of 1 and multiply together to get 12. Since 4 and 3 need to be combined to give us $-x$, we know that the 4 must be negative. These steps would look like this algebraically:

$$x^2 - x - 12 = 0$$
$$(x-4)(x+3) = 0$$
$$x = 4, x = -3$$

In order for the product of $(x - 4)$ and $(x + 3)$ to be 0, we know that x must either be $+4$ or -3 (remember anything times 0 equals 0). So we can confidently say that the parabola crosses the x-axis at $(4, 0)$ and $(-3, 0)$. If you have any shred of interest left at this point, you should graph it to "feel" the symmetry. Now we're going to look at how easy some of these problems can be if you Backsolve.

Quadratic Equations and Backsolving

We know that factoring can be a pain in the neck sometimes, and if the above explanation made your brain hurt, pay close attention to this shortcut. Take the following problem:

Example 1

What are the solutions to the following equation?

$$\left\{ x^2 - 2x - 35 = 0 \right\}$$

A $x = 7, 5$

B $x = -7, -5$

C $x = 7, -5$

D $x = 0, 35$

If you love to factor, go for it. But be aware that there's an even easier way to solve this question—Backsolving (of course). If we plug **A** and **B** back into the equation, we find that only one of the two possible solutions actually solves out to be 0. But with **C**, we find that

$$7^2 - 2(7) - 35 = 49 - 14 - 35 = 49 - 49 = 0!$$
and
$$-5^2 - 2(-5) - 35 = 25 + 10 - 35 = 35 - 35 = 0!$$

That was much easier than the algebra, eh?

Now let's look at a few practice problems—don't forget to Backsolve if you can!

Systems of Equations and Quadratic Equations Drill

1   **Two hamburgers and an order of fries cost $5.50, while 3 hamburgers and an order of fries cost $7.50. What is the cost of a single hamburger?**

    A $1.50

    B $2.00

    C $2.50

    D $3.00

Here's how to crack it:

This is a good word problem example. Backsolve this all the way home. Only $2.00 (**B**) makes all the prices work out correctly. For example, let's try **A** ($1.50) first and see if it works.

$$2h + f = 5.50$$
$$2(1.50) + f = 5.50$$
$$3 + f = 5.50$$
$$f = 2.50$$

Note that we solved the first equation by using $h = \$1.50$, and we got a result $(f = \$2.50)$. Now let's try the second equation and see if it fits.

$$3h + f = 7.50$$
$$3(1.50) + f = 7.50$$
$$4.50 + f = 7.50$$
$$f = 3$$

Nope, **A** doesn't work because the equations solve for *f* differently. Now let's try **B** ($2.00) and solve for the price of the fries using the first equation as so:

$$2h + f = 5.50$$
$$2(2.00) + f = 5.50$$
$$4 + f = 5.50$$
$$f = 1.50$$

So, if the hamburgers really are $2.00, then the fries should be $1.50. We now plug into the second equation to see if it works for both:

$$3h + f = 7.50$$
$$3(2.00) + f = 7.50$$
$$6 + f = 7.50$$
$$f = 1.50$$

Since both equations are solved successfully, **B** must be the right answer!

2   **Solve this system of equations:**

$$\begin{cases} 3x + 4y = 37 \\ 7x - 2y = 41 \end{cases}$$

F $x = 12$, $y = \dfrac{1}{4}$

G $x = 9, y = 11$

H $x = 4, y = 7$

J $x = 7, y = 4$

Here's how to crack it:

Backsolve. Backsolve. Backsolve. Only **J** will work *for both equations*.

3 A line passing through the origin and (−2, 2) will intersect with the line graphed below at what point?

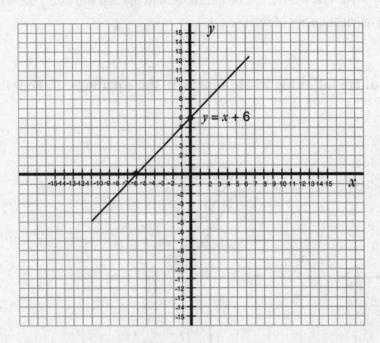

$y = x + 6$

A (3, 3)

B (−3, 3)

C (0, 6)

D (−6, 0)

Here's how to crack it:

This problem can be eyeballed. Sketch the line yourself, and you'll see the intersection should take place while *x* is negative and *y* positive. That eliminates **A** and **C**. Clearly, **B** is the only possible point, as our second line will intersect the first line above the *x*-axis (0).

4 How many solutions does the following system of equations have?

$$\begin{cases} 4x + 3y = 20 \\ 12x + 9y = 60 \end{cases}$$

F 0

G 1

H 2

J Infinite

Here's how to crack it:

This is a tricky question. The same equation is listed twice, with the second equation just multiplied by 3. For that reason, any point that satisfies the first will satisfy the second, and there are an infinite number of solutions, **J**.

5   **Which of the following would represent the equations of the following graph?**

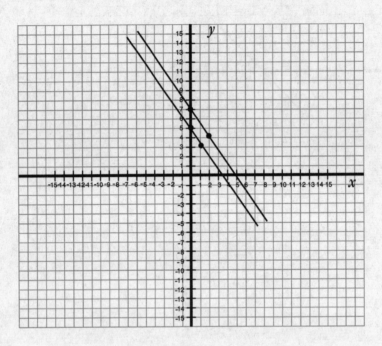

    A $8x + 4y = 20$

           $8x + 4y = 28$

    B $y - 2x = 5$

           $y + 2x = 7$

    C $4x + 2y = 17$

           $4x + 2y = 10$

    D $y - 2x = 7$

           $y - 2x = 14$

Here's how to crack it:

You should immediately notice that the lines are parallel, which means the equations will be the same except for the *y*-intercepts. This observation eliminates **B**, as the equations are different. **D** can be eliminated because the slopes in the graph are negative, while the slope of the equations in answer choice **D** are positive. From there you can either reduce the equation and check the *y*-intercepts, or Plug-In points from the line. Only **A** passes all the tests.

6   In the following figure:

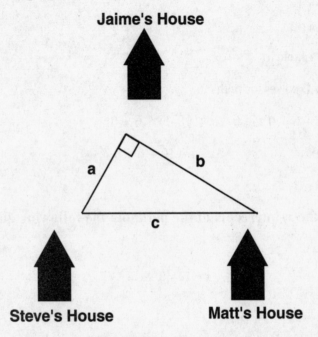

Let *a* be the distance from Steve's house to Jaime's house; and *b* be the distance from Jaime's house to Matt's house. If Steve is going to take a direct route to Matt's house along *c*; and *a* = 60 yards, *b* = 80 yards, and $a^2 + b^2 = c^2$, how far must Steve walk to Matt's house?

F   10 yards

G   100 yards

H   640 yards

J   1000 yards

Here's how to crack it:

Just plug into the quadratic equation and solve. After our work in the last chapter 3, this should be a breeze. $60^2 + 80^2 = c^2$, or $c^2 = 10,000$. The correct answer is **G**, or 100 yards.

7   **What are the *x*-intercepts of the parabola the following quadratic equation creates?**

$$x^2 + 5x + 6 = 0$$

A $x = 3$ or -2

B $x = 3$ or 2

C $x = -3$ or 2

D $x = -3$ or -2

Here's how to crack it:

Backsolve. Only **D** solves for both:

$(-3)^2 + 5(-3) + 6 = 0$ and $(-2)^2 + 5(-2) + 6 = 0$

$9 - 15 + 6 = 0$ $\qquad\qquad\qquad\qquad$ $4 - 10 + 6 = 0$

8   **What are the *x*-intercepts of the parabola the following quadratic equation creates?**

$$6x^2 - x - 12 = 0$$

F $x = \dfrac{-3}{2}$ or $\dfrac{-4}{3}$

G $x = \dfrac{-3}{2}$ or $\dfrac{4}{3}$

H $x = \dfrac{3}{2}$ or $\dfrac{-4}{3}$

J $x = \dfrac{3}{2}$ or $\dfrac{4}{3}$

Chapter 6

Patterns and Functions

Functions are the basic building blocks of higher algebraic reasoning. Simply put, you will need to understand them if you want to pass this test. We'll start with a basic review, and then we'll explore the different aspects of a function that the Algebra I EOC exam will test you on. But before we get to our review of functions, we have to make sure you understand patterns.

Patterns

Identifying patterns is the first step to understanding functions. The Algebra I EOC exam may even ask a few questions based solely on identifying patterns and predicting what numbers they will generate. A mathematical pattern produces a series of numbers by performing specific operations on the numbers in a predictable manner—like adding 5 to each number in a series to produce the next term. The key to identifying patterns is figuring out what operations are repeating, and whether the operations continue to repeat. For example, take the following sequence of numbers:

$$3, 7, 11, 15, 19 \ldots$$

Notice a pattern? If the EOC exam asked you for the number that followed 19, could you provide it? Hopefully, you'd say 23, because that would mean you were able to identify the pattern. In this case, each successive term is deducted by adding 4 to the previous term. Unfortunately, patterns on the actual Algebra I exam can get more complicated. Let's look at another example:

$$0, 1, -1, 1, -2, 1, -3, 1,$$

This pattern is not quite as obvious. In fact, at first glance, it doesn't appear to contain a pattern at all. But let's look a little closer. To get from 0 to 1, we add 1. To go from 1 to -1, we subtract 2. To get from -1 to 1, we add 2. To get from 1 to -2, we subtract 3. So there's a pattern after all, eh? You may have noticed that every other number in the series is 1, but this probably won't be enough to get the question right. The pattern alternates between addition and subtraction; the number added is increased by 1, and the number subtracted will always be one larger than the number added. For all you visual learners, check this out:

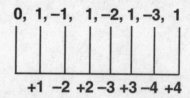

Remember: If you're having trouble spotting the pattern in a series, look for the alternating pattern.

This pattern is more complex because it alternates its operations from term to term. This can be tricky, but the good news is that this is the toughest kind of pattern you'll see on the test.

Before we explore how patterns relate to functions, let's try a few basic examples of identifying patterns. Fill in the missing numbers in each of the following patterns:

1 3, 5, 7, 9, ___

2 2, 5, 8, 12, 16, 21, ___, 32, ___

3 8, 16, 12, 24, 20, 40, 36, 72, ___, 136, ___

4 10, 6, 8, 0, 4, -12, -4, ___, -20, ___

5 10, 5, 15, 7.5, 17.5, 8.25, 18.25, 9.125, ___, ___

Solutions:

1 11 (add 2 to each preceding number)

2 26, 38 (add 3 to each preceding number twice, 4 to each preceding number twice, 5 to each preceding number twice, etc.)

3 68, 132 (multiply by 2, then subtract 4, continue the pattern)

4 −36, −84 (subtract 4, add 2, subtract 8, add 4, continue to double the pattern)

5 19.125, 9.5625 (divide by 2, add 10)

> **Remember:** If you're having trouble spotting the pattern in a series, look for the alternating pattern.

Multiple Patterns: Ordered Pairs, Functions, and Relations

Patterns don't always have to be lonely. Terms in a sequential pattern can be paired with other terms as well. Let's use an illustrative example. Say that Snackeal O'Squeal played in seven basketball games and missed free throws according to the following pattern:

Game #	Free Throws Missed
1	2
2	2
3	4
4	6
5	10
6	16
7	26

Most of us see a chart of free throws, but this is also a list of **Ordered Pairs**, and the EOC exam may ask you about patterns based on these pairs. There's a pattern to Snack's misses, and that pattern manifests itself over the seven games. Look closely at the Free Throws Missed column; can you determine a pattern to his misses? If you examine the column carefully, you'll notice that Snack's free throw misses in each game equal the sum of his misses in his two previous games. The test will expect you to generate ordered pairs from given patterns. Don't worry—this sounds a lot tougher than it is.

For example, given that the pattern holds true, can you predict how many free throws Snack will miss in his 8th and 9th games? Absolutely! And in this process you're doing nothing more than creating ordered pairs that can be graphed. In Snack's 8th game, he should miss the sum of his misses in the two previous games, 16 and 26, or 42. We can write this discovery just like an ordered pair, where our x-coordinate is the game number, and our y-coordinate is the number of misses—such as (8, 42). Take a moment to create an ordered pair indicating how many free throws Snack would miss in his 9th game. The answer is 68 (9, 68).

The ability to spot patterns preludes the much more important skill of identifying functions, both graphically and mathematically. You've already worked with a function above—a function that predicted the number of free throws that Snack will miss. How do we know those ordered pairs make a function? A function is a system of ordered pairs in which each x-coordinate has one and only one y-coordinate. It's that simple. In each game, it's only possible for Snack to miss a single number of free throws.

A *function* is a system of ordered pairs in which each x-coordinate has one and only one y-coordinate. *Relations* are any series of ordered pairs created by two variables.

If the rules of basketball and mathematics were reinvented and somehow Snack missed 6 *and* 8 free throws in a game, these ordered pairs would cease to be a function and become a relation. A relation is any series of ordered pairs created by two variables. Functions can't ever have a repeated x-coordinate in a series of ordered pairs (though the y-coordinate can, like Snack's free throw misses in games 1 and 2); for a relation, anything goes. Any series of ordered pairs listed together forms a relation. To reinforce the difference between a relation and a function, let's look at the following ordered pairs and determine which ones are functions and which are merely relations:

Which of these ordered pairs indicate a function?

1 (5, 7), (3, 5), (–2, 8) (0, 5)

2 (5, 6), (3, 5), (5, 8), (0, 5)

We can just apply the definition of a function—that the x-coordinate will not repeat—to deduce that example 1 is a function. Since two of the ordered pairs in example 2 have x-coordinates of 5, example 2 must be a relation. Now that we've learned to recognize functions, let's examine how they are created, what is the algebra behind them, and how they'll look on a graph.

Functions

Think of a function as a miniature computer program that performs a specific calculation. It works on any number, then spits out a new number based on that calculation. If we want to take a number, add 9 to it, and then divide it by 3, our program would be the function—and we can feed numbers into it and see what it spits out as an output. For example, if we entered 9 into this computer program, what would it do? Let's look at the following visual to see if it helps:

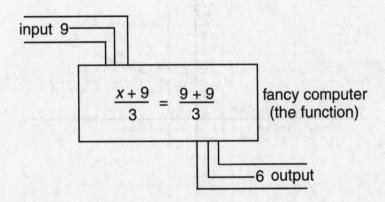

So, our number 9 is plugged into the function for x, where 9 is added to it and then divided by 3. The function then spits out the number 6. Since 9 was fed into the function as the independent variable, it is called the **domain**—and will be represented as the **x-coordinate** on the graph. The 6, since it is the result of the function's calculation, is called the **range**, and it represents the **y-coordinate** of the ordered pair.

We can look at our above graphic and think of our fancy computer as an ordered pair-making machine. When we fed it 9 for x, it gave us 6 for y. Let's feed the machine three more points so that we can represent them on a graph to see what the function looks like. If we input 3, 6, and 0, what would our outputs for each number be? Let's set up a chart and take a look:

input (x)	function	output (y)
9	$\frac{x+9}{3}$	6
3	$\frac{x+9}{3}$	4
6	$\frac{x+9}{3}$	5
0	$\frac{x+9}{3}$	3

So, this function produces the following ordered pairs: $(0, 3)$, $(3, 4)$, $(6, 5)$, and $(9, 6)$. We already know that these points constitute a function because the input (x) differs with every output (y). But there's another test we can use when a function is graphed—the vertical line test. It states that any vertical line should intercept a function at only one point in the graph. Let's plot our ordered pairs from the function above and illustrate the vertical line test.

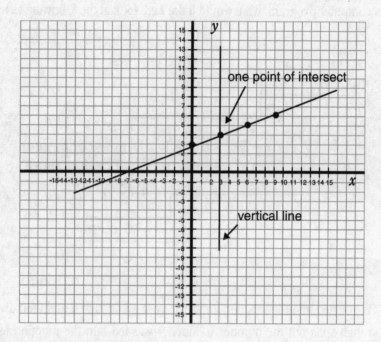

It turns out that our function is linear, because it produced a straight line on the graph. A linear function will always pass the vertical line test, as we've demonstrated above. Any function, when graphed, will intersect a vertical line at exactly one point. In this case, our function intersects the vertical line at $(3, 4)$. An EOC exam question might look like this:

Example 1

Which of the following graphs represents a function?

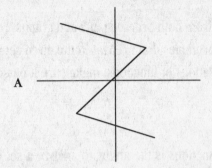

A

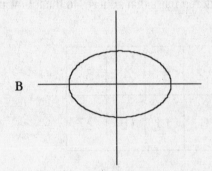

B

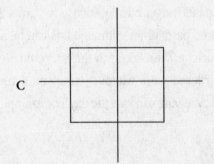

C

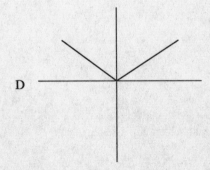

D

The correct answer to this question would be **D**, as it's the only function that a vertical line will intersect only once.

Remember: Functions will cross any vertical line only once.

You need to be able to identify functions from both ordered pairs and graphs. For ordered pairs, make sure that the *x*-coordinates don't repeat in the given set of ordered pairs; for the graphic representations of functions, make sure it passes the vertical line test.

Functions and Backsolving

The last thing you need to become a master of functions is the ability to analyze a set of ordered pairs and find the algebraic function that produced the terms. Finding the pattern becomes key again. Let's say we have a chart of ordered pairs that adheres to the following pattern:

input *(x)*	0	1	2	3	4	5
output *(y)*	2	3	6	11	18	27

Did you notice a pattern? Hopefully, yes. In each case the domain (input) is squared, then 2 is added to it. You may be expected to represent this pattern algebraically, such as $y = x^2 + 2$, or to discern the algebraic function from the ordered pairs given. Although this can be an extremely tricky endeavor, there is an important shortcut. There's no way the test could ever ask you to generate the equation from a set of ordered pairs without giving you a very powerful hint—the answer choices! Once again, Backsolving will save the day. For example, take the following question:

Example 2

The chart below shows how the population of a certain town (P) depends on the number of jobs offered at the local mall (J). Which equation best represents this relationship?

Population (P)	1,000	1,300	1,600	1,900
Mall Jobs (J)	200	300	400	500

F $P = 2J + 600$

G $P = 3J + 400$

H $P = 4J$

J $P = 5J - 100$

This problem sets up a reverse Backsolve—we have variables in the equation, but we can just plug in the numbers from the chart of the function. The pattern must be represented by one of the equations in the answer choices, so the key is to find the equation that works for all of the ordered pairs produced by the chart. But be careful—while all of the answer choices work for some of the ordered pairs, only the right answer will solve correctly for all four sets of numbers. For example, answer choice **F** works for the first equation, but for none of the others. The test-makers would love to catch you being lazy. Only **G** works for all four, and it is the correct answer.

> The test-makers would love to catch you being lazy. Make sure you try all parts of the equation for each answer choice.

Function Presentation

There are only two main ways you'll be expected to identify functions: graphically and through ordered pairs. You already know how to do this. However, the exam will ask questions about functions in different ways. That's why we want you to understand functional notation and how it relates to the domain and range, or the input and output of a function. It's crucial that you recognize the ways that a function can be presented.

Set Notation

One way the domain and range will be presented on the EOC exam is through set notation, which groups all the elements of a domain and range together rather than as ordered pairs. Set notation simply lists the domain and range from the lowest value to the highest, so there is not necessarily a one-to-one correspondence between the domains and range values listed. For example, let's chart a few values of the domain and range of the function $x^2 + 2x + 2$ and then anticipate a few questions that the test could ask regarding set notation.

Domain	Function	Range
−3		5
−2		2
−1	$x^2 + 2x + 2$	1
0		2
1		5
2		10
3		17

The chart above is similar to the other function charts we've looked at, and it produces the following set notation:

$$\text{Domain } \{x: x = -3, -2, -1, 0, 1, 2, 3\}$$
$$\text{Range } \{y: y = 1, 2, 5, 10, 17\}$$

To list the domain and range of a function in set notation, simply list the values of each in numerical order. There are two important characteristics of set notation to remember. First, you *can't* reproduce the ordered pairs as they're graphed from the set notation alone. Since set notation only lists the domain and range in their respective numerical order, you would need either the function or the graph to get the ordered pairs. Second, you *can* determine whether a function exists from set notation alone.

Remember: For every member of a function's range, there must be a unique value for *x*. In our above example, the domain set has no *x*-coordinate repeats, meaning that each *x*-coordinate will be paired with only one *y*-coordinate.

To see an example of set notation that does *not* describe a function, look at the example below:

$$\text{Domain } \{x = 1, 2, 2, 3, 5, 6, 6,\}$$
$$\text{Range } \{y = -2, -4, -5, -7\}$$

We know this does not describe a function because certain values in the domain repeat, meaning that some range values must share a domain value. Set notation will likely only be a component of a more complicated problem. Nevertheless, you need to be very clear on what you can and can't discern from set notation alone, as it could mean the difference between the right and wrong answer.

Functional Notation

Functional notation is the most common (and concise) mathematical way to represent a function, or the correspondence between the values of x and y. Combined with set notation, functional notation provides a complete method to analyze the value and equation of a function. The translation is fairly straightforward, and this is the final concept that you need in order to master the EOC questions generated from these concepts. If we had an algebraic function described by the equation $x^2 + 3x + 5$, we could write this as $f(x) = x^2 + 3x + 5$, which reads: "The value of f at x is $x^2 + 3x + 5$."

So, if we were to evaluate $f(4)$, that would equal $4^2 + 12 + 5$, or 33. We could express this further as $f(4) = 33$, or "the value of f at 4 is 33," or when $x = 4$, y is 33.

If this strikes you as a fancy way to write an ordered pair (4, 33 in this case), you're correct. Once you understand that, it's time to anticipate the types of algebraic questions the EOC exam will tie to functions. There are two main question-types that the test-writers are threatening you with, so let's look at an example of both.

Calculating the Range of Function

A question type you can count on seeing on this exam involves calculating the range of a given function when provided with the domain. To solve, just plug in the domain values for the function and calculate the range. All that's required is that you be familiar with set and functional notation.

Example 3

What is the range of the function $f(x) = x^2 + 5$ when the domain is $\{-2, 5, 6\}$?

A $\{-9, 30, 41\}$

B $\{9, 30, 41\}$

C $\{3, 10, 11\}$

D $\{-3, -10, -11\}$

These questions are a breeze because the test tells you what values to plug in! When we square −2 and add 5, we get 9; when we square 5 and add 5 we get 30; and when we square 6 and add 5 we get 41—giving us **B** as the correct answer. And, since only **B** offered 9 as a possible range, you could tell it was the right answer after solving the range for the domain of −2 (which was 9).

Locating the Zeros of a Function

As with regular algebraic equations, we can manipulate functions to determine where the graph of the function crosses the x- and y-axes. To find where on the graph the function crosses the x-axis, simply set the function equal to 0. To find where the graph crosses the y-axis, simply plug in 0 to the function's variable and see what value results. Take the following function, $f(x) = x^2 - 9$, and find the x and y zeros of the function. First, we'll find the x-intercepts using functional notation by setting the equation equal to 0, just as we reviewed in chapter 4:

$$f(x) = x^2 - 9 = 0$$
$$f(x) = (x + 3)(x - 3) = 0$$
$$\text{so}$$
$$f(-3) = 0 \text{ and } f(3) = 0$$

Remember: What we put into the function is our x-coordinate, and what the function spits out is our y-coordinate. We want to know what value(s) of x give us 0. In this case, by identifying the equation as the difference of 2 squares, we can quickly determine that the input (x) of 3 and −3 will give us 0 as the output (y). To find the y-intercept, we want to know what the equation equals when x is 0, so we just plug in:

> What we put into the function is our x-coordinate, and what the function spits out is our y-coordinate.

$$f(x) = x^2 - 9$$
$$f(0) = 0^2 - 9$$
$$f(0) = -9$$

So, here we have a parabola that intercepts the x-axis at 3 and −3, and hits the y-axis at −9.

Let's try an example:

Example 4

Locate the zeros of the *x*- and *y*-axes of the following function:

$$f(x) = x^2 + 2x - 35$$

F *x*: -7, 5 / *y*: -35

G *x*: 7, -5 / *y*: -35

H *x*: -7, 5 / *y*: 35

J *x*: 35 / *y*: -7, 5

Remember: To find the zero for *x*, set the equation to 0. To find the zero for *y*, find f (0).

It is very easy to find the zero-coordinate for *y*, because you just find the value of the function when *x* is 0: $f(0) = 0^2 + 2(0) - 35 = -35$. This eliminates **H** and **J**. Now we can Backsolve, and find that when *x* is −7 or +5, the equation equals 0, leaving **F** as the right answer. For all you factoring fanatics out there:

$$f(x) = x^2 + 2x - 35 = 0$$
$$f(x) = (x = 7)(x - 5) = 0$$
$$\text{so}$$
$$f(-7) = 0$$
$$f(5) = 0$$

Variations

There are two major mathematical relationships that describe how *x* will change with *y*. Direct and indirect variations demonstrate the proportion between the variables, and there are two simple formulas to make this clear. Memorize the following formulas for the variations, and you will be glad you did when you're taking the EOC Algebra I exam.

Direct Variations: $y = kx$

A direct variation is a relationship between x and y in which **y increases as x increases**. You may see a problem on the Algebra I EOC exam that uses wording like "y varies directly with x". This relationship is described algebraically as $y = kx$, where k represents the constant by which the relationship is increasing. The graph of a direct variation is a straight line that passes through the origin, (notice the above equation lacks a y-intercept, so we can assume it's 0), but the easiest way to visualize the relationship is as a proportion. The test will expect you to be able to look at a table of information and determine whether a direct variation exists. You may also be expected to solve for certain values given that a direct variation exists.

The key to cracking both types of questions lies in the ability to set up a proportion to find the constant (k), or the factor by which the variation is increasing. For example, if we were to say the y varies directly with x, and that when x is 7, y is 14, we could solve for the constant by plugging into the direct variation equation, $y = (k)x$. We would then determine by what constant the equation increases. Let's try it:

> The graph of a direct variation is a straight line that passes through the origin.

$$14 = (k)7$$

$$\frac{14}{7} = \frac{7k}{7}$$

$$k = 2$$

Now that we know the constant (2), making predictions about other values in the variation is easy. To get y, multiply x by 2. What would the value of y be if x were -10? If you said -20, you'd be right on ($-10(2) = -20$). Now try a quick sample question.

Example 5

The following chart represents the distance a car traveled over a certain interval on a trip during spring break:

Hours Driven (y)	Miles Traveled (x)
2	180
3	270
4	360

How many miles would the car have traveled after 6 hours if the car maintained a constant speed?

A   450

B   480

C   530

D   540

The term "direct variation" is never mentioned, but you will be expected to know the problem is based on direct variation solely from data in the chart. A direct variation is pretty easy to visualize, because the y-element will increase as x increases. We hope you noticed that the Miles Traveled column (y), increased proportionally to the value of Hours Driven(x). That's the basis of direct variation. Also, when x is 0 (hours), y is 0 (miles), producing an ordered pair of (0, 0), or the origin. This speed demon's constant speed was 90 miles an hour, making our correct answer **D**.

Inverse Variations: $y = \dfrac{k}{x}$

An inverse variation is a relationship between x and y in which **x is increased as y is decreased**, and vice versa. Fancy word problems will use language like "y varies indirectly with x," and test will expect you to plug into the equation $y = \dfrac{k}{x}$. Again, you will be expected to recognize this type of variation from charts alone. You will always be able to solve for a value when given three points in an inverse variation. Memorizing the formula is the key. Let's take a look at a chart representing an inverse variation and see if we can make a few predictions based on what we find there.

Example 6

The following chart represents the amount of money Carol earns per hour and her corresponding amount of days off:

Days Off (y)	Hourly Wage (x)
10	24
8	30
6	40

Based on the above relationship, how much free time would Carol have if she earned \$120 per hour in the month of October and was required to take at least one day off?

F   1 day

G   2 days

H   3 days

J   4 days

Memorization is the key. Say the formulas for direct and indirect variations aloud 100 times, if it helps you remember.

Remember: In an inverse variation, y will decrease as x increases. The more money Carol earns, the less time she has off, indicating an inverse variation. Just as with a direct variation, the key is to solve for the constant (k), so we can compute additional points on the chart.

Since the days off are getting smaller, we'll assign them y and plug into the equation $y = \dfrac{k}{x}$, picking any two points from the chart. For simplicity, we'll pick the first and solve for the constant—giving us the equation $10 = \dfrac{k}{24}$. Multiplying both sides through by 24, we determine our constant (k) to be 240, which allows us to solve for the number of days off in the question. Memorize the formula, solve for the constant, then you can provide any point. In this case, we'd plug into the formula as follows:

$$y = \frac{240(k)}{120(x)}$$

So she'll make a lot of money per hour, but get only two days off, or **B**.

Functions and Variations Drill

1   **Which of the following represents the omitted term in the following pattern?**

$$32, 16, 64, 32, 128, 64, \_\_\_, 128, 512$$

A   32

B   128

C   256

D   512

Here's how to crack it:

The key to cracking patterns is to spot the repetitive operation(s). Patterns with multiple operations will likely appear on the exam, and the above question is a good example. The pattern repeats between dividing the first term by 2 and then multiplying the resulting quotient by 4. 128 was divided by 2 to give us 64, so we need to multiply 64 by 4 to come up with 256, or **C**, the correct answer.

2   **The following is the list of a domain and range from a certain function. Which of the following equations could represent the algebraic operation this function performs?**

Domain (x)	4	9	16	25	36	49
Range (y)	3	4	5	6	7	8

F $y = x^2 + 1$

G $y = \dfrac{x}{2} + 1$

H $y = \dfrac{x}{5} + 1$

J $y = \sqrt{x} + 1$

Here's how to crack it:

It's critical to know the difference between the domain and range. So we plug in for x and see which numbers result for y. Notice that the wrong answer choices will work for one or two of the pairs of elements for the domain and range, but only **J** works for all the ordered pairs—making it the right answer.

3 The following chart represents the number of refugees $\{r\}$ that leave their home country based on the number of tons of rice $\{t\}$ the country imports from abroad.

Tons of Rice Imported (t)	20	50	70	100
Number of Refugees (r)	10,600	25,600	35,600	50,600

Which of the following equations best represents this relationship?

A $\quad r = 450t + 1{,}600$

B $\quad r = 450t + 3{,}100$

C $\quad r = 500t + 600$

D $\quad r = 550t + 600$

Here's how to crack it:

The last thing you should do is to try to deduce the equation by looking at the chart. Attack the answer choices. Only one equation will work for *all* of the data in the chart. That equation is represented by answer choice **C**, and we can confirm this answer by Plugging In the numbers given in the chart.

4 What is the range of the function $f(x) = x^2 + 4$ when the domain is $\{-2, 5, 7\}$?

F $\{-8, 29, 53\}$

G $\{8, 29, 53\}$

H $\{8, 9, 169\}$

J $\{8, 25, 49\}$

Here's how to crack it:

Plug the domains into the function, and the ranges will be spat out. Note that the domain and range are always listed from smallest to biggest, so there won't necessarily be a one-to-one correspondence between the domain and range. Only **G** spits out all the values of the function.

5 At what points does the graph of this function intersect the x- and y-axes?

$$f(x) = x^2 + 14x + 49$$

A $x: (x = 7, 0)$ $y: (y = 49, 0)$

B $x: (x = 0, 7)$ $y: (y = 0, -49)$

C $x: (x = 0, -7)$ $y: (y = 0, 49)$

D $x: (x = -7, 0)$, $y: (y = 0, 49)$

Here's how to crack it:

A quick scan of the answer choices is a big help because we know that y must equal 0 at the x-intercept, meaning that **B** and **C** can be crossed out immediately. We also know that x must equal 0 at the y-intercept, meaning that only **D** has the zeros where they need to be, so it must be the right answer. But, for all you algebra buffs, here's how we'd solve: Set the function equal to zero to find the x-intercepts like so: $x^2 + 14x + 49 = 0$. We hope you recognize this equation as quadratic, which breaks down like so: $(x + 7)(x + 7) = 0$, meaning that x must be -7 when y is 0. For the y-intercept, set x to 0, and you get 49—or $(y = 0, 49)$.

6   At what points does this function cross both the *x*- and *y*-axes?

$$f(x) = x^3 - 2x^2 - 24x$$

F   *x*: {*x* = 0, –4, 6}; *y*: {*y* = 0}

G   *x*: {*x* = 0, 4, –6}; *y*: {*y* = 0}

H   *x*: {*x* = 0, –4, –6}; *y*: {*y* = 0, 10}

J   *x*: {*x* = 0}; *y*: {*y* = 0, 10}

Here's how to crack it:

Backsolve! Let's scan the *y*-coordinates first. All of the answer choices contain 0 as a zero-intercept, but **H** and **J** both have 10 as well. If this function zeros at 10 (or if it doesn't), we can cross out two choices immediately! To check if the function crosses the *y*-axis at 10, we set the *x*-coordinate to 0 and find that it gives us $0^2 - 2(0)^2 - 24(0) = 0$, and 0 only, meaning 10 is *not* a point on the *y*-axis where the function crosses. So **H** and **J** are gone. Now we could set the function to 0, factor, and solve for the *x*-intercepts. Or we could continue to attack the answers. What are the differences between **F** and **G**? **F** has *x*-intercepts of –4 and 6, while **G** has *x*-intercepts of 4 and –6. All we need to do is Backsolve them into the equation and find which one equals 0, as so:

F: $-4^3 - 2(-4)^2 - 24(-4) = -64 - 32 + 96 = 0$

The –4 gives us our 0, so we don't even have to check answer choice **G**. It's **F**.

7   If *y* varies directly with *x*, and *y* is 36 when *x* is 24; what is *y* when *x* is 72?

A   27

B   54

C   108

D   216

Here's how to crack it:

For direct variation, the formula is $y = kx$, where k is the constant. So, let's plug in the pair that we know has the variation and then solve for the constant:

$$y = kx$$
$$36 = k(24)$$
$$\frac{36}{24} = k\frac{24}{24}$$
$$k = 1.5$$

Since our constant is 1.5, let's apply it to our value for x and then solve for y:

$$y = 1.5(72)$$
$$y = 108$$

The answer is **C**. The constant (k) is the key to all direct and indirect variation questions.

8 **If y varies indirectly with x, and y is 18 when x is 7, what is y when x is 21?**

   F 6

   G 12

   H 27

   J 54

Here's how to crack it:

The formula for indirect variation is $y = \dfrac{k}{x}$, with k as our faithful constant. Remember, with indirect variations, y decreases as x increases, so we know that **H** and **J** must be wrong (because they get larger). Let's solve for the constant:

$$18 = \frac{k}{7}$$
$$(7)18 = (7)\frac{k}{7}$$
$$126 = k$$

With our constant, we can solve for the pair in question:

$$y = \frac{126}{21}$$

$$y = 6$$

The correct answer is **F**.

9 **The following chart relates the average number of minutes (m) spent by a college admissions officer reviewing each college application received (n).**

number of applications recieved (n)	minutes spent per application (m)
100	10
200	5
300	$3\frac{1}{3}$
400	$2\frac{1}{2}$

If (n) continues to vary indirectly with (m), how many minutes would the officer spend if the school received 500 applications?

A   20

B   10

C   2

D   1.5

Here's how to crack it:

First, do a little estimating. Clearly, the time spent is getting smaller—so with 500 applications, we know the total must be less than 2.5, which is how long the college admissions officer spent on each application with 400 applicants. This eliminates **A** and **B**. Solve for the constant k, which should give you 1000 ($100 = \dfrac{k}{10}, k = 1000$), and then we can plug the constant back in and solve for 500 apps: $500 = \dfrac{1000}{m}, m = 2$, so **C** is our correct answer.

Chapter 7

Statistics

Of the 50 questions that will be scored on your Algebra I EOC exam, only eight will be taken from the reporting category of statistics. Nevertheless, some of the skills from this reporting category can get complicated, so we're going to explain every statistical procedure in detail and present you with practice questions. There are three major skills you need to know to master statistics—and get all eight questions right on the exam. Let's start with the least complex of the three statistical skills, *the matrix*. But don't expect Keanu Reeves to lend any assistance on this project!

Matrices

Remember set notation from the last chapter? Set notation expresses the domain and range of a function in sequential order, clearly laying out the function's data. Matrices have the same goal as set notation—to present mathematical elements in an organized manner. Unlike set notation, however, matrices are not limited to one row of data. Matrices are composed of **rows** and **columns**. Rows move horizontally and columns run vertically—meaning we can broadly define a matrix as **a rectangular array of numbers enclosed by brackets**. Let's take a look at an example, so that we can demonstrate the critical parts of a matrix:

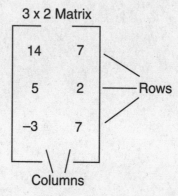

Unlike set notation, a matrix uses rows *and columns* of mathematical data.

True to its definition, the matrix above has a set of numbers in a rectangular array, enclosed in brackets. The **dimensions** of a matrix are conveyed by listing the number of rows multiplied by the number of columns. In the above matrix, there are three rows and two columns, making it a 3×2 matrix. The multiplication symbol shows how many **elements** are contained within the matrix—3 times 2, or 6.

The EOC exam will expect that you can locate specific elements based on their placement in the matrix. One important thing to remember is that *the row will always be listed first*. For example, what number is in row 2, column 2, of the above matrix? Counting from the top for the rows and from the left for the columns, 2 is the number in row 2, column 2. The number in row 3, column 2, is 7.

Matrices on the Exam

Matrices on the exam are mostly going to list information taken from everyday life. For example, they may list a series of book prices at different locations for a local bookstore in matrix form, as follows:

	Hardcover	Paperback	
Location 1	$20	$6	Matrix (P)
Location 2	$25	$13	Retail Prices at 3 Locations for the Novel
Location 3	$32	$11	**"In the Beauty of the Lilies"**

On the Algebra I EOC exam, there won't be any matrices with dimensions larger than 4 × 4!

A matrix works like a chart, and the above example tells us the retail price for hardcover and paperback versions of *In the Beauty of the Lilies*, for three locations. We have a 3×2 matrix—we'll call it matrix (P), for price—listing the locations in the rows and the type of book in the columns.

Matrices can get tricky when the test asks you to manipulate its values by a given operation or operations. Say that all three locations are in the same state, and that this state charges a 6% sales tax on each book sold. The test may ask you to select a matrix that represents the amount of the tax on each book. In essence, we'll create a new matrix by multiplying all the elements of the original matrix by 6%, or .06. So, the dimensions of the new matrix will be the same as our original matrix, and each value in the new matrix will correspond to the values in the same row and column of the old matrix. We'll elaborate a little with the following demonstration:

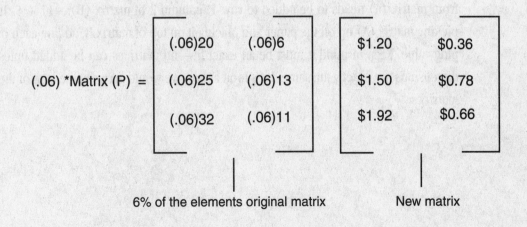

(.06) *Matrix (P) =	(.06)20	(.06)6		$1.20	$0.36
	(.06)25	(.06)13		$1.50	$0.78
	(.06)32	(.06)11		$1.92	$0.66

6% of the elements original matrix   New matrix

In the original matrix, row 1, column 1, the price of the hardcover book was $20. In our new matrix, row 1, column 1 contains $1.20, or the 6% sales tax assessed to the $20 book. So in our new matrix (we'll call it (T) for tax), we have the sales tax for each corresponding book from matrix (P). You will probably see a question on the test like this, where you're asked to perform a specific operation on an existing matrix. Just remember to keep the same order for both matrices and perform the same operation to each element, and you'll do fine. Now, let's peek at matrix addition and subtraction.

Matrix Addition and Subtraction

If you followed the example on the previous page, adding and subtracting matrices will be a breeze. To add or subtract two matrices, you simply combine the corresponding elements of each matrix based on the operation. Let's say you wanted to add the two following matrices:

$$
\begin{bmatrix} 23 & 5 & 21 \\ -17 & 11 & 13 \\ 42 & 87 & -6 \end{bmatrix} + \begin{bmatrix} 0 & 1 & 3 \\ 5 & 4 & 5 \\ 3 & 7 & 7 \end{bmatrix}
$$

Matrix (A)   Matrix (B)

In the above example, we have two 3×3 matrices that we want to add together. The corresponding values of each matrix need to be added. In other words, row 1, column 1 of matrix (A) needs to be added to row 1, column 1 of matrix (B), or 23 + 0. Then row 1, column 2 from matrix (A) needs to be added to row 1, column 2 of matrix (B): −17 + 5. Imagine picking matrix (A) up off the paper and placing it on top of matrix B, adding each overlapping value. Keep in mind it must be an exact fit—no matrices can be added unless their dimensions are exactly the same. Let's look at how we would arrive at the sum of the above matrices:

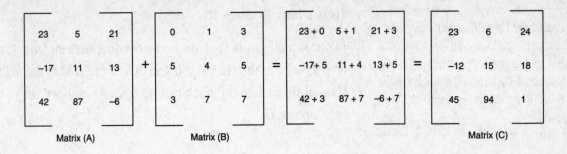

23	5	21		0	1	3		23 + 0	5 + 1	21 + 3		23	6	24
−17	11	13	+	5	4	5	=	−17 + 5	11 + 4	13 + 5	=	−12	15	18
42	87	−6		3	7	7		42 + 3	87 + 7	−6 + 7		45	94	1

Matrix (A)   Matrix (B)   Matrix (C)

So, our original two matrices (A and B) are combined by adding each corresponding element to create a final matrix, (C), which represents the sum of the two matrices. Pretty easy, huh? Matrix subtraction works exactly the same way, except we *subtract* the second matrix from the first matrix. Still pretty easy, huh? Try an example involving matrix subtraction:

> No matrices can be added unless their dimensions are exactly the same.

Example 1

The following two matrices represent the stock and sales of a certain companies' goo-goo doll collection for the Month of May, 2000:

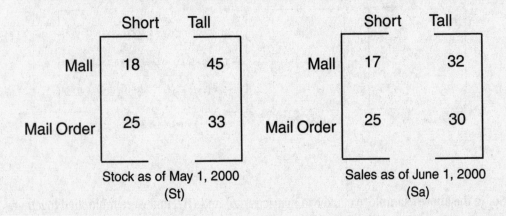

	Short	Tall
Mall	18	45
Mail Order	25	33

Stock as of May 1, 2000
(St)

	Short	Tall
Mall	17	32
Mail Order	25	30

Sales as of June 1, 2000
(Sa)

How many tall goo-goo dolls are available at the mall?

A   0

B   1

C   13

D   3

Here's how to crack it:

In our second matrix (Sa), the corresponding element (row 1, column 2) tells us that 32 tall goo-goo dolls were sold at the mall in May. All we have to do is subtract 32 from 45, and we've got our right answer, **C**.

Matrix Multiplication

The other operation involving matrices that you will expect to know is the multiplication of matrices, otherwise known as scalar multiplication. You'll still need to be familiar with the rows and columns of the matrices, but the method needed to solve these questions is less straightforward than with matrix addition and subtraction. **Matrix multiplication** involves multiplying the elements of the first matrices' row by the second matrices' column elements. The **sum** of these products will make up the elements of the resulting answer matrix. Let's use an example to demonstrate this process:

$$
\begin{bmatrix} 4 & 2 & 1 \\ 6 & -3 & 4 \\ 0 & 5 & 6 \end{bmatrix} \cdot \begin{bmatrix} 3 & 1 \\ 5 & 3 \\ 2 & 4 \end{bmatrix} = \begin{bmatrix} (4 \cdot 3)+(2 \cdot 5)+(1 \cdot 2) & (4 \cdot 1)+(2 \cdot 3)+(1 \cdot 4) \\ (6 \cdot 3)+(-3 \cdot 5)+(4 \cdot 2) & (6 \cdot 1)+(-3 \cdot 3)+(4 \cdot 4) \\ (0 \cdot 3)+(5 \cdot 5)+(6 \cdot 2) & (0 \cdot 1)+(5 \cdot 3)+(6 \cdot 4) \end{bmatrix} = \begin{bmatrix} 24 & 14 \\ 11 & 13 \\ 37 & 39 \end{bmatrix}
$$

Matrix (A)   Matrix (B)   Answer Matrix (C)   Matrix (C)

So, in the above example, we had two matrices, (A) and (B), that were multiplied together. Notice that all the values of *row* 1 in Matrix A were multiplied by their corresponding elements in *column* 1 of Matrix B, then added together to give us Matrix C. The mixing, by multiplication and addition, of rows and columns can make this process very tricky. Make sure you're solid on the differences between matrix addition and matrix multiplication.

Central Tendency

Central tendency describes specific points in a set of data that tell us where the "middle" lies in a given set of numbers. There are three important terms that describe different aspects of central tendency—the mean, the mode, and the median. After we've thoroughly reviewed these concepts, we'll show you the format of central tendency that you will be expected to know on the EOC exam.

Average or Arithmetic Mean

The first key term of central tendency is **average** or **arithmetic mean**, and this figure is arrived at by dividing the sum of a set of numbers by the number of elements in that set. You've probably done this when trying to figure out your grade in a class. For example, say that Suzie Greenberg took ten tests in her Algebra I course, and her results were as follows:

Suzie Greenberg's Test Results (tests 1-10): {87, 81, 76, 70, 68, 82, 82, 85, 88, 84}

To find Suzie Greenberg's average, we need to add up all of her test scores and then divide by the number of tests she took—in this case, 10. Her average would be the result.

Suzie Greenberg's Average: $\dfrac{87+81+76+70+68+82+82+85+88+84}{10} = \dfrac{803}{10} = 80.3$

An average is the sum of all of the elements of a set of numbers divided by the number of elements in the set.

Mode

A second important term that may appear on the EOC exam is **mode**, which is the term that appears the most in a set of numbers. Referring to Suzie Greenberg's grades, can you determine which number in the set appears the most? Keep in mind, we're not looking for the largest number (which would be 88), but the number that *appears most often*. In this case, 82 appears twice, more than any other number—making it the mode.

Median

Finally, the term **median** means middle or the term that falls directly in the middle of a set of numbers. We need to list numbers in a set in sequential order (i.e., smallest to largest) to determine the median of the set. Let's look at a simple example, conveniently listed in sequential order below:

$$\text{Set (A) } \{23, 43, 50, 52, 55\}$$

What number falls in the middle? It's 50, of course, making it the median. Now determine the median of Suzie Greenberg's test results from our previous example.

In Suzie Greenberg's case, she has ten test scores, so no single score falls exactly in the middle:

$$\{68, 70, 76, 81, 82, 82, 84, 85, 87, 88\}$$

When given a set with an even number of figures, we need to look at the **two** terms that fall directly in the middle and take their average. In this case, both numbers are 82, so their average is easy to figure out—it's just 82! If you had two different numbers fall in the middle then you would average the two different numbers. Take the following set for an example:

$$S = \{12, 14, 16, 19\}$$

In this case both 14 and 16 fell in the middle, so we'd take their average to find the median:

The mean is the average of a set of numbers; the mode is the number that appears most often; and the median is the number that falls in the middle.

$\dfrac{14+16}{2} = \dfrac{30}{2} = 15$. Let's try a sample question that involves all three terms.

Example 2

The following set of numbers represents the results (in inches) from a recent frog-jumping contest for five different contestants:

$$\{10.8, 11.1, 9.5, 11.1, 12\}$$

Which of the following sets represents the average, median, and mode, respectively, for the results of the frog-jumping contest?

A   {10.8, 9.5, 11.1}

B   {10.8, 9.5, 11.1}

C   {10.9, 11.1, 11.1}

D   {10.9, 11.1, 12}

> It may help you to remember that *mode* and *most often* both start with "*mo.*" Also, *median* and *middle* have the same number of letters.

Here's how to crack it:

To find the average, just add up the numbers and divide by 5 (the number of elements in the set). That gives us $\dfrac{10.8+11.1+9.5+11.1+12}{5} = \dfrac{54.5}{5} = 10.9$ as our average. Mode means occurring the most, which is 11.1, as it occurs twice, once more than any other element in the set. Finally, when we list the numbers in order, {9.5, 10.8, 11.1, 11.1, 12}, we find that 11.1 falls directly in the middle. **C** puts these values in their correct order, making it the right answer.

Box-and-Whisker Graphs

Box-and-Whisker is one of two types of statistical graphs you will be expected to be comfortable with on the Algebra I EOC exam. The **Box-and-Whisker Graph** is designed to convey central tendency, and identifying the median is a very important part of getting Box-and-Whisker questions correct. Fortunately, we've just reviewed median, so now we can take a detailed look at how Box-and-Whisker graphs are constructed. We'll also review how questions on the EOC exam will be based on them.

A Box-and-Whisker graph conveys information about all the elements in a particular set, whereas the average, median, and mode give a more limited picture of central tendency. A Box-and-Whisker graph illustrates the highest and lowest numbers in a set, the median, and at what points the majority of elements fall. Let's take Suzie Greenberg's test results, list them in order, and then construct a Box-and-Whisker graph based on the results.

Test Results: {68, 70, 76, 81, 82, 82, 84, 85, 87, 88}

Box and Whisker Graph:

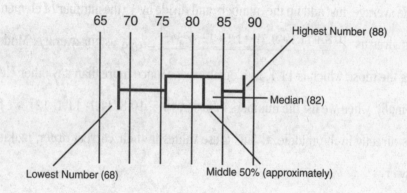

Now the term "Box-and-Whisker" makes a little more sense, eh? The "Box" demonstrates where roughly half of the all numbers in the set fall (in this case there were 10 elements, so we included the middle six numbers). The "Whiskers" demonstrate the highest and lowest numbers in the set, in this case 68 and 88. And finally, the line drawn within the box indicates the median. The questions on the EOC exam will be fairly straightforward—as long as you remember those rules.

For most Box-and-Whisker questions, start with the highest and lowest numbers in a given set, since they will be the easiest to identify. That will usually eliminate a couple of answer choices. For the remaining choices, identify the median and determine the Box-and-Whisker graph that correctly indicates the median. We'll look at an actual example below, after we review the Stem-and-Leaf Charts.

Stem-and-Leaf Charts

The second statistical format the exam will test you on is called a **Stem-and-Leaf Chart**—another way to convey set and element information in a sequential order. Think of a Stem-and-Leaf chart as splitting two-digit numbers in half, with the stem as the tens digit, and the leaf as the ones digit. For example, if we had the number 84, the stem would be 8, and 4 would be the leaf.

Stem-and-Leaf charts become convenient when trying to convey a large amount of data, like Suzie Greenberg's test results. Referring to her chart, we notice that Suzie had several test scores in the 80s, and these scores could be rewritten in a Stem-and-Leaf chart with 8 as the stem (or tens digit) and each score conveyed as a leaf (the ones digit of each score). The resulting chart would look as so:

Suzie's Test Scores in the 80s: (81, 82, 82, 84, 85, 87, 88)

STEM	LEAF
8	1224578

As you can see, these can look incredibly confusing—especially because the graph doesn't put a space between the results under the Leaf category. Let's look at the rest of Suzie Greenberg's test data and use it to build a complete sample Stem-and-Leaf graph:

Test Results: {68, 70, 76, 81, 82, 82, 84, 85, 87, 88}

Stem	Leaf
6	8
7	06
8	1224578

The "stems" 6, 7, and 8 represent the tens digits of all the numbers in the set. The "leafs" are the ones digits of each number that begins with the respective stem. The numbers in the "leaf" column are bunched together and look like one large, ugly number. The trick to these graphs is recognizing each digit in the leaf column as completing a number from the stem column. In the "leaf" column of the stem of 7, we have 06. When each digit is tacked onto the stem, it becomes clear that this row conveys the 70 and 76 from Susie Greenberg's test scores.

Since these charts will always be listed in order, it's very easy to find the median. The median is the middle number, so we simply look for the digit or digits that fall directly in the middle. There is one digit in row 6, two digits in row 7, and seven digits in row 8. Look at the graphic below:

Stem	Leaf
6	8
7	06
8	1224578

Notice how we crossed out the highest and lowest numbers, highlighting the median. You don't need to list all the numbers out to find a median, simply work your way into the middle by canceling out high and low values, as we've done above. Cross off the lowest number, then cross off the highest number; keep repeating until you have one or two numbers left. When the higher and lower values were crossed out, we were left with two "2s" in the middle of the 8 stem, making 82 our median.

The Median-Fit Graphing Method

We spent a lot of time looking at graphs of linear equations in chapter 4. The skills we reviewed in that chapter will be very important in understanding what the Median-Fit Method is trying to accomplish, and what you will be expected to do with given information. First, let's generate a set of data so that we have a framework from which to understand the Median-Fit graphing method.

Not all statistical information fits neatly into a specific pattern. Take the scoring averages and heights for a certain women's high school lacrosse team:

Height	Scoring Average
59"	1
60"	4
60"	3
62"	2
63"	6
64"	2
66"	7
68"	6

Look familiar? If the term "ordered pairs" comes to mind, that's good. We can graph these pairs to determine the relationship between the values. We already know this set of ordered pairs does not represent a function. Why not? There are two 5' players with different scoring averages, and a domain can never repeat in a function. In this case, our x value, or domain, had two 60" (5-foot tall) players.

Since this data is rather scattered, the technical name for this data's graph is a **Scatterplot**. Scatterplots won't make a straight line when graphed, because the data they represent doesn't have a linear relationship (the points will literally look "scattered" about the graph). The Median-Fit method offers a way to make predictions about the scoring averages of other members of the team based on the "scattered" nature of the data.

The points in a scatterplot reflect data that isn't linear. Its points will be scattered, and the Median-Fit method is designed to find the average line of all the scattered points.

Essentially, the Median-Fit method finds the two points that fall in the middle of the scattered points (thus the name median) and connects those two points with a line. This line gives us a general predictive tool of future points since it slices the scattered points down the middle, giving us a median line to make predictions. Let's plot the points above and see what two points fall in the middle:

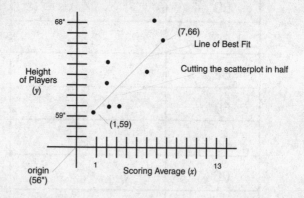

Our goal is to find the line that puts the same number of points above and below the line. The line needs to go through two of our existing points, and its fancy name is the **Line of best fit.** In the above example, when we drew a line between (1, 59") and (7, 66"), the line put three points above the line and three points below the line. That's our line of best fit. It's as simple as that.

We can turn this line of best fit into a linear equation and make predictions about the scoring averages of future lacrosse players. Take our two points and create an equation of a line below. Recalling chapter 4, we first find the slope between our two points as so:

$$\frac{rise}{run} = \frac{66 - 59}{7 - 1} = \frac{7}{6} = slope$$

With our slope, we need to take one of the two coordinates and solve for the y-intercept. Remember the equation of a line? It's $y = mx + b$. We already know the slope (m) is $\frac{7}{6}$. By plugging in our point $(1, 59)$, we get the following:

$$59 = \frac{7}{6}(1) + b$$

$$59 = \frac{7}{6} + b$$

$$59 - \frac{7}{6} = b$$

$$\frac{354}{6} - \frac{7}{6} = b$$

$$\frac{347}{6} = b$$

So, the equation of the line created by the two points that cut the plot of points in half is $y = \frac{7}{6}x + \frac{347}{6}$. We can confirm this by checking the other ordered pair, $(10, 7)$; it plugs into this equation perfectly:

$$66 = \frac{7}{6}(7) + \frac{347}{6}$$

$$66 = \frac{49}{6} + \frac{347}{6}$$

$$66 = \frac{396}{6} = 66$$

The EOC exam most will likely limit their questions of scatterplots to identifying the equation of the line of best fit. Your steps to solve this kind of question are as follows: First, identify the two points that cut the scatterplot in half. Second, formulate the linear equation these two points create.

Keep in mind that, of all the categories on the exam, you can expect to see the least number of problems from this chapter. Most likely, you'll only get one or two Median-Fit questions. Nevertheless, we want you to squeeze out every possible point. And since the exam is untimed, you should be able to nail these questions down. Pay close attention to the following drill to see how the exam will ask the statistic category questions.

Statistics Drill

1   **The following matrices represent the points scored by four different players on two nights.**

	Game 1		Game 1
Player 1	5	Player 1	0
Player 2	7	Player 2	4
Player 3	3	Player 3	5
Player 4	2	Player 4	7

Which matrix represents the total points for the four players on both nights?

A	B	C	D
5	5	50	0
3	11	74	28
−2	8	35	15
−5	9	27	14

Here's how to crack it:

The key to this problem is picking up from the wording of the question that they want you to *add* the two matrices. Adding each corresponding element gives you the matrix **B**, the sum of each row. Note this matrix has dimensions of 4×1.

2   Which of the following represents the product of the following two matrices?

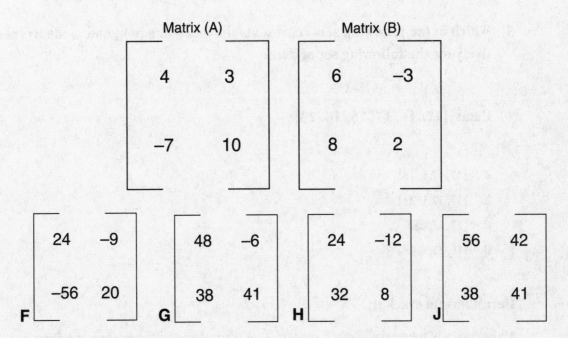

Matrix (A)

$$\begin{array}{cc} 4 & 3 \\ -7 & 10 \end{array}$$

Matrix (B)

$$\begin{array}{cc} 6 & -3 \\ 8 & 2 \end{array}$$

F. $\begin{array}{cc} 24 & -9 \\ -56 & 20 \end{array}$
G. $\begin{array}{cc} 48 & -6 \\ 38 & 41 \end{array}$
H. $\begin{array}{cc} 24 & -12 \\ 32 & 8 \end{array}$
J. $\begin{array}{cc} 56 & 42 \\ 38 & 41 \end{array}$

Here's how to crack it:

Watch out for **F**! Unlike addition and subtraction, matrix multiplication does not simply combine corresponding elements! ***Remember:*** You multiply the row elements of the first matrix by the column elements of the second. You then add each product together for your answer matrix. For example, 4 and 3 of row 1 in Matrix A are multiplied by 6 and 8 from column 1 of matrix B. 4 times 6 is 24, and 3 times 8 is 24. The sum of these products is 48, which should be row 1, column 1 of the correct matrix. Since only **G** has 48 in this spot, it must be the right answer.

Matrix (A)   Matrix (B)

$$\begin{bmatrix} 4 & 3 \\ -7 & 10 \end{bmatrix} \cdot \begin{bmatrix} 6 & -3 \\ 8 & 2 \end{bmatrix} = \begin{bmatrix} 4 \bullet 6 + 3 \bullet 8 & 4 \bullet -3 + 3 \bullet 2 \\ -7 \bullet 6 + 10 \bullet 8 & -7 \bullet -3 + 10 \bullet 2 \end{bmatrix} = \begin{bmatrix} 48 & -6 \\ 38 & 41 \end{bmatrix}$$

3 **Which of the following sets represents the mean, median, and mode, respectively for the following set of data?**

Data: {12, 14, 17, 18, 18, 23}

A   {17, 17.5, 18}

B   {17. 17.5, 23}

C   {17, 17, 23}

D   {16, 17.5, 18}

Here's how to crack it:

Make sure you memorize these three terms! As we reviewed above, **mean** is a fancy word for average, so we'd add the six terms together and divide by the number of terms, giving us 17 ($\frac{12+14+17+18+18+23}{6} = \frac{102}{6} = 17$). That only eliminates **D**, since **A**, **B**, and **C** all have 17 as the average. The **median** is the number that falls directly in the middle when the terms have been listed in order. In this case, the median is tricky because there are an even number of terms, meaning no one number falls precisely in the middle. The average of 17 and 18, the two numbers that fall in the middle, is 17.5, meaning **C** cannot be the right answer. **Mode** means "most," as in appears the most, *not* has the most value. Since 18 appears twice, it's the mode, making **A** the correct answer.

4 Which Box-and-Whisker graph best represents this Stem-and-Leaf plot?

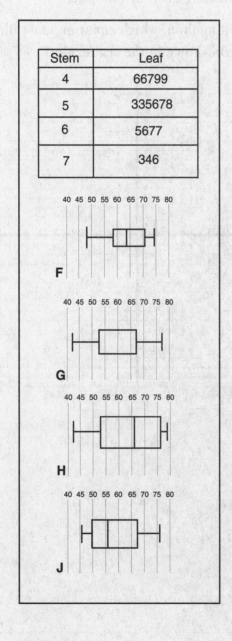

Stem	Leaf
4	66799
5	335678
6	5677
7	346

> **Remember:** We average the *two* terms that fall precisely in the middle to find the median in this case.

Here's how to crack it:

Box-and-Whisker and Stem-and-Leaf graphs look much scarier than they really are. The Stem-and-Leaf graph merely lists all the elements of a set by placing the tens digit as the stem and the different ones digits as the leaves. In our above example, a stem of 4 with leaves of 66799 means that we have 46, 46, 47, 49, and 49 in our set. So this Stem-and-Leaf's highest number is 76, and its lowest is 46. 56 and 57 fall directly in the middle of our stem and leaf, making our median 56.5. Finally, 49 and 67 roughly mark the upper and lower 25% of the data. Roughly half the numbers fall between 49 and 67, making it the "box." **J** reflects all of these statistical tendencies, making it our correct answer.

5 **Using the Median-Fit method, which equation most likely represents the line of best fit for the data shown in the scatterplot?**

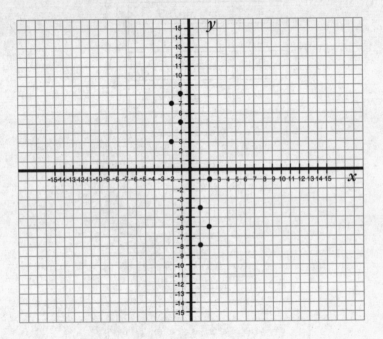

A $y = \dfrac{x}{2}$

B $y = x + 4$

C $y = \dfrac{-13x}{4} + \dfrac{1}{2}$

D $y = -8x + 2$

Here's how to crack it:

This question is practically begging to be Backsolved. Median-Fit questions can be a real pain-in-the-you-know-what, so attacking the answer choices can provide an easier solution. First things first. In general, the points seem to be declining as you move from left to right. This indicates that the slope of our line of best fit must be negative. Say goodbye to **A** and **B**. To decide between **C** and **D**, simply sketch both lines on the graph. They should look like so:

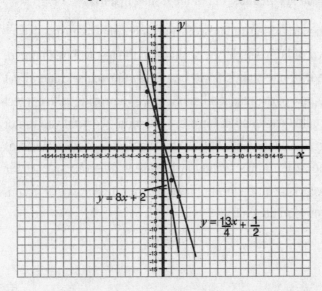

The only question left is: Which line has an equal number of points on both sides of the equation? Only **C**. That's how we take a complicated question and crack it wide open!

Practice-Test Heaven

Well, that's it! We've covered every item that the Virginia EOC Algebra I exam will test you on. To evaluate your understanding of these skills, we've written two complete practice exams based on the content that Virginia Department of Education says it will test you on. Don't worry, you're ready. Before taking the exams, brush up on any question-type you may be rusty on, so you can get the most out of the testing material.

Each test is 60 questions long and is broken up according to the categories the Virginia Board of Ed has published. Although the test will be untimed, you have to take it in one sitting. So to be true to the actual exam, don't break the test up into parts; take it all at once! We've provided the correct answer and a detailed explanation for every question. We want you to not only practice your test-taking skills but also find any last-second weaknesses that you'll need to work on. It's been our pleasure to help you prepare for this exam, and we wish you the best of luck on your Algebra I EOC exam. But, of course, you won't need it.

> **Remember:** The actual exam will have 10 "Field Test" questions that won't count toward your final score. Unfortunately, you won't know which are the "real" questions, so you'll have to answer them all.

Chapter 8

Practice Test 1

Note: On the actual End-of-Course Algebra I SOL exam, you may see a weird negative symbol. Instead of the usual −7, you will probably see a ⁻7. Minus signs will still look the same, such as $5x − 3y − 9$. But negative numbers will look like ⁻9. Don't let it fool you.

1 Solve the following linear equation for x:

$$5x - 4 = 3x + 30$$

    A −17

    B −13

    C 13

    D 17

2 x and y are integers that must satisfy the following conditions:

$$x > 80$$
$$y < 70$$

What is one possible value for $x - y$?

    F 0

    G 5

    H 10

    J 12

3 Solve the following inequality for x:

$$4x + 7 > 3x - 5$$

    A $x < -12$

    B $x > -12$

    C $x < -2$

    D $x > -2$

4 A TV network charges for advertising time for their hit series "Bakersfield 90218" according to the following formula:

$$c = \frac{v}{100} \cdot \frac{1}{t} \cdot m$$

Where c is the cost, v is the number of viewers, t is the number of times the show has aired, and m is the length in minutes of the commercial.

What is the cost of a 90218 commercial that is 2.5 minutes long, has aired twice, and has 2,000,000 viewers?

    F $2,500

    G $25,000

    H $50,000

    J $75,000

5 What is the multiplication inverse of

$$\frac{4y - 3}{x}$$

    A $\dfrac{x}{4y - 3}$

    B $\dfrac{y}{x}$

    C $\dfrac{3}{4}y - x$

    D $\dfrac{4}{3}y - x$

6 Which of the following expressions is equal to 5(17) + 5(83)?

    F (17 + 5) (17 + 83)

    G 5(17 + 83)

    H 495

    J 505

7 Which of the following ordered pairs would be produced by the equation
$$-6x + 5 = 5y?$$

    A (–5, 7) and (0, 1)

    B (5, –7) and (0, 1)

    C (–5, 7) and (1, 0)

    D (5, –7) and (1, 0)

8 What is the equation of the following line?

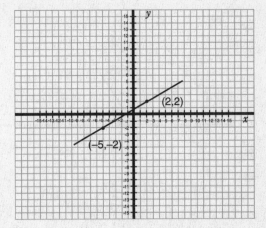

    F $y = \dfrac{2}{5}x - 4$

    G $y = -\dfrac{4}{7}x + \dfrac{6}{7}$

    H $y = \dfrac{4}{7}x + \dfrac{6}{7}$

    J $y = \dfrac{4}{7}x - \dfrac{6}{7}$

9 Which of the following lines are represented by the function $y = -3x + 2$?

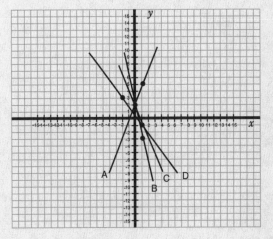

10 What is the slope of the line in the following graph?

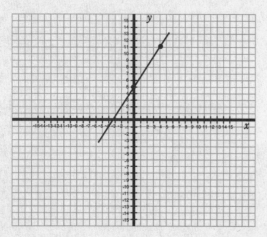

    F −2

    G −1.5

    H 1.5

    J 2

11 What is the *x*-intercept of a line that has a *y*-intercept of 7 and a slope of −4?

    A $\dfrac{-7}{4}$

    B $\dfrac{-4}{7}$

    C $\dfrac{4}{7}$

    D $\dfrac{7}{4}$

12 Which of the following lines would be the graph of $y = x + 4$ if the slope were doubled?

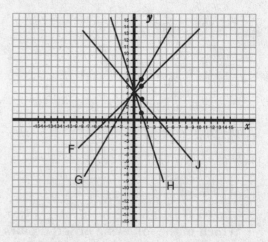

13 What is the solution to this system of equations?

$$\begin{cases} y - 7 = -4x \\ x - 8 = y \end{cases}$$

    A $x = 0, y = \dfrac{-4}{7}$

    B $x = 1, y = 3$

    C $x = 3, y = -5$

    D $x = 5, y = -3$

14 What is the solution to this system of equations?

$$\begin{cases} 2x = y + 1 \\ 3y = 5x + 1 \end{cases}$$

    F $x = 0, y = -1$

    G $x = 4, y = -7$

    H $x = 4, y = 7$

    J $x = 6, y = 11$

15 The price of two tickets and one Coke at the Columbus Astros' baseball game is $11.00. The price of three tickets and two Cokes is $17.00. How much is <u>one ticket</u> to an Astros' baseball game?

A $2.50

B $5.00

C $6.50

D $7.50

16 A line passing through the origin and (–6, 8) will intersect with the line graphed below at what point?

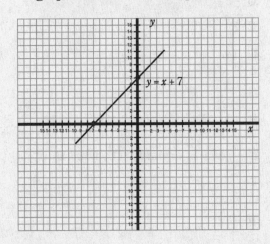

F (3, 3)

G (–3, 4)

H (–3, 8)

J (–6, 0)

17 What are the x-intercepts of the parabola the following quadratic equation creates?

$$x^2 - 5x - 14$$

A $x = 7$ or -2

B $x = 7$ or 2

C $x = -7$ or 2

D $x = -7$ or -2

18 What are the solutions to the following equation?

$$\left\{ x^2 + 12x + 32 = 0 \right\}$$

F $x = -8, 4$

G $x = -8, -4$

H $x = 8, 4$

J $x = 8, 0$

19 What is the result of $5\sqrt{3} \cdot 3\sqrt{3}$?

A $8\sqrt{3}$

B $15\sqrt{3}$

C 30

D 45

20 $\dfrac{5^3 \cdot 5^8}{10^3} =$

    F $\dfrac{5^8}{10}$

    G $2 \cdot 5^8$

    H $2 \cdot 5^5$

    J $\dfrac{5^{11}}{10^3}$

21 A certain computer can make $1.8 \cdot 10^4$ calculations per second. At this rate, how many calculations will the computer make in $3.6 \cdot 10^8$ seconds?

    A $6.48 \cdot 10^2$

    B $6.48 \cdot 10^{\frac{1}{2}}$

    C $6.48 \cdot 10^{12}$

    D $6.48 \cdot 10^{32}$

22 What is the value of $\dfrac{7x^2 - 5y + 2}{y + 3}$, if $x = 2$ and $y = 6$?

    F -24

    G -12

    H -6

    J 0

23 What is the value of $-2x + 8 - xy^2$ if $x = -2$ and $y = 1$?

    A -14

    B -8

    C 8

    D 14

24 If $\dfrac{4}{5}$ of x is equal to 16, what is x?

    F 4

    G 8

    H 16

    J 20

25 A certain baseball player demands that his salary equal $\frac{1}{10}$ of his team's total revenue, plus $\frac{1}{2}$ of all the popcorn sold during each game. If his team's revenue was \$350,000 and \$7,000 of popcorn was sold during each game, how much is the ballplayer demanding to be paid?

A \$3,500

B \$7,000

C \$35,000

D \$38,500

26 If $a = (2x + y)$ and $b = (4z + xy)$, what is $a \cdot b$?

F $8xz + 2x^2y + 4zy + xy^2$

G $8xz - 2x^2y - 4zy - xy^2$

H $6xyz - 2xy - 4z$

J $6xy + 2xy + 4y^2$

27 If $c = (x + y)$ and $d = (x + y)$, what is $c \cdot d$?

A $2x + 2y$

B $x^2 + y^2$

C 1

D $x^2 + 2xy + y^2$

28 Simplify the following expression:
$5xy^2 + (xy + 5) + xy^2 + (3xy - 6)$

F $5x^2y^2 + 4xy - 6$

G $6xy^2 + 4xy - 1$

H $5xy^2 + 5xy - 18x^2y$

J $10xy + 18xy^2$

29 Factor completely: $x^2 - 7x - 18$

A $(x - 2)(x - 9)$

B $(x + 2)(x - 9)$

C $(x - 7)(x + 9)$

D $(x + 7)(x + 9)$

30 Which of the following represents in $\dfrac{x^2 - 2x - 15}{x^2 + x - 6}$ its completely factored form?

F $x - 5$

G $x - 2$

H $\dfrac{x - 2}{x - 5}$

J $\dfrac{x - 5}{x - 2}$

31 The following chart represents the total pounds of pollution (p) that country t produces, based on the number of cars the country imports (c).

Pounds of Pollution (p)	20	50	70	100
Number of Cars (c)	14,000	20,000	24,000	30,000

Which of the following equations best represents this relationship?

A $c - 8,000 = 300p$

B $c - 10,000 = 200p$

C $c = 400p$

D $c - 3,000 = 300p$

32 Which of the following represents the omitted term in the following pattern?

$$2, 12, 24, 34, 68, 78, \_\_\_, 166 \ldots$$

F 88

G 128

H 156

J 165

33 The following chart represents the total investment (i) that country t receives based on its compliance with the number of international banking laws (l).

# of laws complied with {l}	10	15	20	25
Total Investment {l}	10,500	15,500	20,500	25,500

Which of the following equations best represents this relationship?

A $i = 1000(l) + 500$

B $i = 2000(l) - 14,500$

C $i = 300(l) + 11,000$

D $i = 400(l) + 12,500$

34 What is the range of the function $f(x) = \dfrac{x^3 + x^2 + x}{2}$ when the domain is {−4, −2, 1}?

F $\{-26, 3, \frac{3}{2}\}$

G $\{-26, -3, \frac{3}{2}\}$

H $\{26, 3, \frac{3}{2}\}$

J $\{52, 6, \frac{1}{2}\}$

35 What is the domain of function $f(x) = 5x^2 + x$, if the range is {22, 84, 130}?

   A {−2, 4, 5}

   B {−2, −4, 5}

   C {2, 4, 5}

   D {2, 22, 7, 84, 17, 130}

36 At what x- and y-coordinates does this function cross the x- and y-axes?

$$f(x) = x^3 - 2x^2 - 8x$$

   F x: {$x = 0, 2, 4$}; y: {$y = -8$}

   G x: {$x = 0, -2, 4$}; y: {$y = 0$}

   H x: {$x = 0, -2, -4$}; y: {$y = -8$}

   J x: {$x = 0$}; y: {$y = 0, -8$}

37 If $f(x) = x^2 - 2x + 5$, then what is the value of $f(8)$?

   A 47

   B 50

   C 53

   D 56

38 At what points does the graph of this function intersect the x- and y-axes?

$$f(x) = x^2 - 6x + 9$$

   F x: ($x = -3, 0$) y: ($y = 9, 0$)

   G x: ($x = 0, 3$) y: ($y = 0, -9$)

   H x: ($x = 0, -3$) y: ($y = 0, 9$)

   J x: ($x = 3, 0$), y: ($y = 0, 9$)

39 If y varies indirectly with x, and y is 14 when x is 7, what is y when x is 42?

   A $2\dfrac{1}{3}$

   B 21

   C 84

   D 98

40 Of the following sets of ordered pairs, expressed as domain (*x*) and range (*y*) which set represents a function?

F Domain {–1, 5, 7, 7}

Range {1, 25, 79, 144}

G Domain {2, 4, 6, 6}

Range {1, 9, 13, 17}

H Domain {–1, 1, –2, 2}

Range {2, 5}

J Domain {2, 2, 3, 4, 4, 5}

Range {2, 4, 6, 8, 10, 12}

41 Which of the following graphs does NOT represent a function?

A
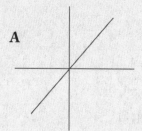

B
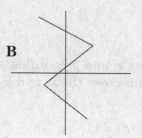

C
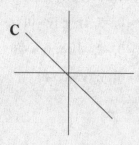

D
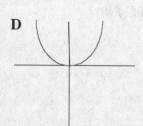

42 The following chart represents the relationship between the dollars spent by a certain political lobbyist ($), and the number of favorable laws passed by the Congress for his company (l):

Lobbying $ Spent ($)	# of Favorable Laws (l)
$10,000	20
$50,000	100
$100,000	200
$500,000	1,000

If (l) continues to vary directly with ($), how many favorable laws would be passed for the lobbyist's company if he spent $1,000,000?

F 2,000

G 2,200

H 2,400

J 2,500

43 The following matrix represents the number of hits that two professional baseball players made against right and left-handed pitchers:

	Alan	Dale
Left	315	665
Right	714	543

If each player had four times as many at bats as hits against both right and left-handed pitchers, then which matrix accurately reflects their number of at bats?

A

	Alan	Dale
Left	315	665
Right	714	543

B

	Alan	Dale
Left	1260	2660
Right	2856	2172

C

	Alan	Dale
Left	1260	1350
Right	2800	1086

D

	Alan	Dale
Left	630	1330
Right	1028	1086

44 What is the sum of the following two matrices?

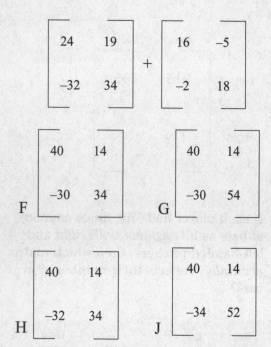

$$\begin{bmatrix} 24 & 19 \\ -32 & 34 \end{bmatrix} + \begin{bmatrix} 16 & -5 \\ -2 & 18 \end{bmatrix}$$

F $\begin{bmatrix} 40 & 14 \\ -30 & 34 \end{bmatrix}$

G $\begin{bmatrix} 40 & 14 \\ -30 & 54 \end{bmatrix}$

H $\begin{bmatrix} 40 & 14 \\ -32 & 34 \end{bmatrix}$

J $\begin{bmatrix} 40 & 14 \\ -34 & 52 \end{bmatrix}$

45 The following two matrices represent the stock and sales of a clothing store's pairs of pants for the Month of May, 2000:

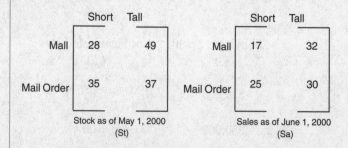

	Short	Tall
Mall	28	49
Mail Order	35	37

Stock as of May 1, 2000 (St)

	Short	Tall
Mall	17	32
Mail Order	25	30

Sales as of June 1, 2000 (Sa)

How many total pairs of pants are available at this particular store in the mall?

A 11

B 17

C 28

D 32

46 Which of the following sets represents the average, median, and mode, respectively, for the following set of numbers?

$$\{6.7, 5.2, 4.8, 6.7, 8\}$$

F {6.25, 5.2, 6.7}

G {6.25, 5.2, 8}

H {6.28, 6.7, 8}

J {6.28, 6.7, 6.7}

47 Which of the following represents the product of the following two matrices?

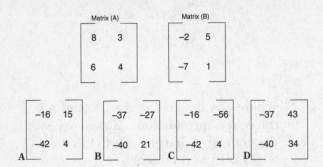

Matrix (A)

8	3
6	4

Matrix (B)

−2	5
−7	1

A
−16	15
−42	4

B
−37	−27
−40	21

C
−16	−56
−42	4

D
−37	43
−40	34

48 The following stem-and-leaf chart shows the age of the employees of company *x*. According to the chart, what is the median age of the employees of company *x*?

Stem	Leaf
1	88899
2	0114689
3	1122567
4	00126
5	00345

F 3

G 32

H 35

J 36

49 Which box-and-whisker graph best represents this stem-and-leaf plot?

Stem	Leaf
2	22588
3	113467
4	6799
5	256

A

20 25 30 35 40 45 50 55 60

B

20 25 30 35 40 45 50 55 60

C

20 25 30 35 40 45 50 55 60

D

20 25 30 35 40 45 50 55 60

50 Using the Median-Fit method, which equation most likely represents the line of best fit for the data shown in the scatterplot?

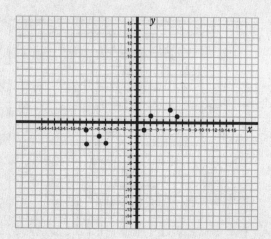

F $y = \dfrac{x}{4} - 5$

G $y = \dfrac{x}{4} + \dfrac{1}{2}$

H $y = 4x + \dfrac{1}{2}$

J $y = 4x + 5$

51 If y varies directly with x, and x is 7 while y is 10, what is y when x equals 10?

A 7

B 14

C $14\dfrac{2}{7}$

D 20

52 A record company prices CDs using the following formula:

$$c = \dfrac{p}{10,000}(1.5) + 11.00$$

Where c is the cost of the CD and p is the cost of production. How much will the company charge for a CD that cost $100,000 to produce?

F $2.60

G $6.50

H $13

J $26

53 Given that: $f(x) = x^3 + x - 7,$

What is the value of $f(5)$?

A 23

B 53

C 123

D 246

54 If $4x + 7y = 12$, and $2x + 5y = -10$, then what is the value of $x + y$?

F –10

G 11

H 12

J 22

55 A certain monkey can only nurse her offspring according to the following temperature (t) conditions:

$$225 > 3t > 246$$

Which of the following answer choices simplifies the monkey's nursing temperature preference?

A $70 > t > 80$

B $75 > t > 82$

C $77 > t > 84$

D $79 > t > 86$

56 John's weight is twice that of Mary's. Also, if Mary's weight were subtracted from John's, the result would be 200 pounds. Which of the following is Mary's weight?

F 100

G 200

H 300

J 400

57 Line x, not shown, has a slope of $\dfrac{-2}{5}$. If $(-2, 5)$ and $(3, z)$ are points on line x, what is the value of z?

A 0

B 1

C 2

D 3

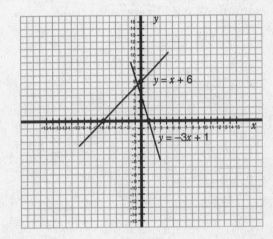

$y = x + 6$

$y = -3x + 1$

58 Which of the following would be the product of the slopes of the two lines drawn above?

F –5

G –3

H 0

J 3

59   What is the value of $x^2 + 2xy + y^2$, if x is 4 and y is -3?

   A -1

   B 0

   C 1

   D 2

60   If $f(2) = 7$, which of the following equations could represent $f(x)$?

   F $x^3 - 1$

   G $x^3 - 2$

   H x^4

   J $x^2 + 2$

Chapter 9

Practice Test 1 Answers and Explanations

1 **D**

2 **J**

3 **B**

4 **G**

5 **A**

6 **G**

7 **A**

8 **H**

9 **C**

10 **H**

11 **D**

12 **G**

13 **C**

14 **H**

15 **B**

16 **G**

17 **A**

18 **G**

19 **D**

20 **F**

21 **C**

22 **J**

23 **D**

24 **J**

25 **D**

26 **F**

27 **D**

28 **G**

29 **B**

30 **J**

1   **D**   **Here's how to crack it:** The building block of algebra—and this test— is solving a linear equation. Remember the two rules: Isolate the variable and solve for x. Remember, whatever we do to one side, we do to the other. First, let's add 4 to both sides:

Original equation: $5x - 4 = 3x + 30$

$$5x - 4 \ (+ \ 4) = 3x + 30 \ (+ \ 4)$$
$$5x = 3x + 34$$

Next, we need to isolate the variable by subtracting $3x$ from both sides as so:

$$5x \ (-3x) = 3x \ (-3x) + 34$$
$$2x = 34$$

Finally, we need to solve for a single x by dividing both sides by 2:

$$\frac{2x}{2} = \frac{34}{2}$$
$$x = 17$$

Don't take this test without being confident in your ability to solve a linear equation. This problem shouldn't be difficult for you by now; go back and review chapter 4 if you had any problems with it. And if you were at all unsure of the correct answer, you could always Backsolve. By putting the answers back into the original equation, only 17 (**D**) solves for x perfectly.

2   **J**   **Here's how to crack it:** The easiest way to solve this question is to plug in values according to the conditions given. x must be larger than 80 and y must be less than 70, and the smallest integer larger than 80 is 81, and the biggest integer less than 70 is 69.

Subtract the second from the first and you get 12, or answer **D**. Note there's no number we could plug in to get 10, let alone 5 or 0.

3   B   Here's how to crack it: Solve inequalities just as you would linear equations. Subtract 7 from both sides of the original equation, $4x + 7 > 3x - 5$, and you should get

$$4x + 7 \, (-7) > 3x - 5 \, (-7)$$
$$4x > 3x - 12$$

Then, subtract $3x$ from both sides, and you get the correct answer:

$$4x \, (-3x) > 3x \, (-3x) - 12$$
$$x > -12$$

4   G   Here's how to crack it: Read carefully, and plug in the numbers where the formula wants them plugged in! When you plugged in, it should have looked like this:

$$c = \frac{2,000,000(v)}{100} \bullet \frac{1}{2(t)} \bullet 2.5(m) =$$
$$20,000 \bullet \frac{2.5}{2} = 25,000$$

You should use your calculator for this one.

5   A   Here's how to crack it: This question is just a question of algebraic terms. A multiplication inverse is just the fraction flipped upside down, which is exactly what A is in relation to the question. Remember, a number times its inverse always equals 1.

6   G   Here's how to crack it: A calculator is one way to solve this problem, just make sure your calculator knows PEMDAS. The sharp student will recognize the distributive property in this question, and can save time by picking G. You should be able to recognize the distributive property at all times. Check back with chapter 3 if you don't remember the rules of these properties.

31	**B**
32	**H**
33	**A**
34	**G**
35	**C**
36	**G**
37	**C**
38	**J**
39	**A**
40	**H**
41	**B**
42	**F**
43	**B**
44	**J**
45	**C**
46	**J**
47	**D**
48	**G**
49	**A**
50	**G**
51	**C**
52	**J**
53	**C**
54	**G**
55	**B**
56	**G**
57	**D**
58	**G**
59	**C**
60	**F**

If you Backsolved this problem, you would see that only choice **G** equals 500, which is what $5(17) + 5(83)$ is equal to.

7   **A** **Here's how to crack it:** Now Backsolving rears its head! The key to this question is to attack the answers! Only the correct answer will have BOTH points plug successfully into the equation. Only A works with both points. Answering this problem the old-fashioned way takes unnecessary time and effort.

$$(-5, 7)$$
$$-6x + 5 = 5y$$
$$-6(-5) + 5 = 5(7)$$
$$30 + 5 = 35$$

$$(0, 1)$$
$$-6x + 5 = 5y$$
$$-6(0) + 5 = 5(1)$$
$$5 = 5$$

8   **H** **Here's how to crack it:** Backsolve again. Even with the big fancy graph, there's no real difference between question 7 and question 8. Plug the two points on the graph into each equation, the correct answer will work for both. Notice with **H**:

$$y(2) = \frac{4}{7}x(2) + \frac{6}{7} \quad \text{and} \quad y(-5) = \frac{4}{7}x(-2) + \frac{6}{7}$$

In both of these equations, y equals x, so it's the right answer.

You can tell from the graph that the y-intercept is a little above 0. So just by looking at the answer choices, you can eliminate **F** and **J**, both of which have negative y-intercepts. And since **G** has a negative slope (and the slope of the line in the graph is positive), only **H** remains as a choice. Sometimes you don't need to do any more work than this.

9   **C** **Here's how to crack it:** There's an easy procedure. First, we know the y-intercept must be +2 if we've understand the equation of a line. That eliminates **D**, because it's not intercepting the y-axis at 2. Next check whether the slope is positive or negative.

Remember, a *positive* slope will go *up* from left to right, a *negative* slope will go *down*. Our slope is –3, yet answer choice A is positive, meaning it must be wrong. Since our slope is –3, every time x increases by 1, y should drop by 3. We can eyeball **B** and see that it's dropping much more than three spaces. **C** must be our right answer.

10 H Here's how to crack it: Let's start with whether our slope is positive or negative. It's positive, right? So **F** and **G** must be gone. From there, count the rate of change. Point 1 is at (0, 5), point 2 at (4, 11). So, as x increased by 4, y jumped by 6. Remember slope as Rise/Run, in this case $\frac{6}{4}$, and you have **H**, 1.5.

11 D Here's how to crack it: You need to know the equation of a line (chapter 4 again, eh?).

$y = mx + b$. Where m is the slope (rise/run) and b is the y-intercept. Plugging In the numbers from above, that leaves us with:

$$y = -4x + 7$$

We don't have the answer quite yet. The trick to this question is identifying that at the x-intercept, y must equal 0. We Plug In 0 for y, and simply solve for the equation:

$$0 = -4x + 7$$
$$4x = 7$$

$$\frac{4}{4}x = \frac{7}{4}$$

$$x = \frac{7}{4}$$

12 G Here's how to crack it: Know your equation for a line! The slope in our initial equation was 1, so doubled, it's 2. **H** and **J** are negative slopes, so they can be eliminated immediately. Only G increases y by 2 with an increase of 1 in x.

13 C Here's how to crack it: If you remember from our subject review, there are at least three ways to solve systems of equations. We're going to encourage Backsolving, because it's the easiest. We want the answer choice that provides the numbers that successfully plug into BOTH equations, $y - 7 = -4x$ and $x - 8 = y$

If you try **B**, you get $3 - 7 = -4$ (correct) and $1 - 8 = 3$ (incorrect). So **B** would be wrong.

Watch with **C**:

$$-5 - 7 = -4 \ (3)$$
$$-12 = -12 \ (\text{correct})$$

$$3 - 8 = -5$$
$$-5 = -5 \ (\text{correct})$$

14 H Here's how to crack it: Backsolve. Put the answer choices back into the original equations, and see which ordered pair fits correctly for both. Only **H** solves for both.

$$2 \ (4) = 7 + 1 \text{ and } 3 \ (7) = 5(4) + 1$$
$$8 = 8 \ (\text{correct}) \text{ and } 21 = 21 \ (\text{correct})$$

15 B Here's how to crack it: You need to translate the word problem into an equation, then solve the systems of equations:

$$2 \text{ tickets plus 1 Coke is } \$11.00 : \ 2t + c = 11.00$$
$$3 \text{ tickets plus 2 Cokes is } \$17.00 : \ 3t + 2c = 17.00$$

From here, you can use substitution, or addition and subtraction. In this case, substitution is the least complicated route:

$$2t + c = 11.00$$
$$\text{or}$$
$$c = 11.00 - 2t$$

Now that we know what c is $(11 - 2t)$, plug it into the other equation. That way we can solve for a single t:

$$3t + 2c = 17.00$$
$$3t + 2(11.00 - 2t) = 17.00$$
$$3t + 22.00 - 4t = 17.00$$
$$-t + 22.00 \ (-22.00) = 17.00 - (22.00)$$
$$-t = -5.00$$
$$t = 5.00$$

Tricky, but manageable, right?

16 G Here's how to crack it: Graph the new line! This is a good example where a quick sketch would quickly lead you to the right answer. You don't have to be perfect. Drawing a line through the origin to (–6, 8) creates a line like so:

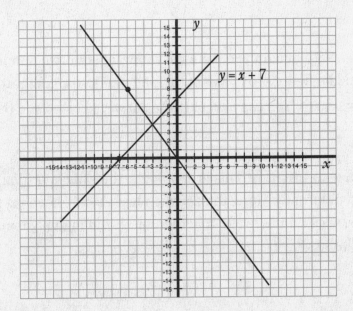

From here, you can visually verify the point of intersection as (–3, 4) or **G**. This answer could be double-checked using simultaneous equations, but the test's graphs will be drawn to scale, so draw you graph carefully and you'll get your right answer!

$$y = x + 7$$
$$-(y = -\frac{4}{3}x)$$
$$\overline{\quad\quad\quad}$$
$$0 = \frac{7}{3}x + 7$$
$$\overline{\quad\quad\quad}$$
$$-\frac{7}{3}x = 7$$
$$x = -3$$

$$y = x + 7$$
$$y = -3 + 7$$
$$y = 4$$

17 A Here's how to crack it: Don't bother graphing this out. For the x-intercepts you simply set the equation equal to 0 and solve.

$$x^2 - 5x - 14 = 0$$
$$(x + 2)(x - 7) = 0$$
$$x = -2, \text{ or } 7$$

Remember, with quadratic equations, you want your two numbers to add together to get the middle figure (–5 in this case), and multiply together to get the end figure (–14 in this case). You can also plug the answer choices into the

18 G Here's how to crack it: This is essentially the same question as 17, but they are presented differently. Here, the equation has already been set to 0, so you need to determine what numbers add together for 12 and multiply together for 32. It ends up looking like so:

$$x^2 + 12x + 32 = 0$$
$$(x + 8)(x + 4) = 0$$

Since one of the two parentheses has to equal 0, we know x must be –8 or –4.

You could also just plug the numbers in the answer choices into the original equation, and see which gives a result of 0 for both numbers.

19 D Here's how to crack it: Combine like terms of $5\sqrt{3} \cdot 3\sqrt{3}$ through multiplication.

$$5 \cdot 3 = 15,$$
$$\sqrt{3} \cdot \sqrt{3} = 3$$
$$15 \cdot 3 = 45$$

It's that simple.

20 F Here's how to crack it: Know your exponent rules (covered in chapter 3) by heart. To multiply exponents, you ADD the exponents together, giving you $\dfrac{5^{11}}{10^{3}}$.

The correct answer is **J**.

21 C Here's how to crack it: Remember scientific notation? Just follow your laws of exponents and multiply like terms together. $1.8 \bullet 3.6 = 6.48$, and $10^{4} \bullet 10^{8} = 10^{12}$. 6.48×10^{12} is the correct answer.

22 J Here's how to crack it: Plug In! The equation in the numerator equals out to 0, giving you $\dfrac{0}{9}$, or 0, for **J**.

$$\frac{28 - 30 + 2}{9} = \frac{0}{9} = 0$$

23 D Here's how to crack it: Again, Plug In!

$$-2(-2) + 8 - (-2)1 = 4 + 8 + 2 = 14$$

24 J Here's how to crack it: Translate and solve.

$$\frac{4}{5}x = 16$$
$$\frac{5}{4}\left(\frac{4}{5}x\right) = 16\left(\frac{5}{4}\right)$$
$$x = 20$$

You don't even need to perform the math on this problem, since you know that if a little less than x is 16, x must be more than 16. And only **J** is over 16.

25 D Here's how to crack it: Read carefully and plug in the numbers properly into the equation. $\frac{1}{10}$ of the $350,000 revenue is $35,000, and $\frac{1}{2}$ of the popcorn is $3,500. Add them together for $38,500.

26 F Here's how to crack it: Know FOIL by heart! First, Outer, Inner, Last. The algebra should look like this:

$$(2x + y)(4z + xy)$$
$$8xz \,(\text{first}) + 2x^2y \,(\text{outer}) + 4yz \,(\text{inner}) + xy^2 \,(\text{last})$$

27 D Here's how to crack it: FOIL again. This should be considered an essential identity and memorized. Who knows how the test could reward a student who memorized this equality?

28 G Here's how to crack it: Combine like terms. Here we are only adding or subtracting, so there's no hierarchy of operations. We'll rewrite the equation now with the like terms next to one another:

$$5xy^2 + xy^2 + xy + 3xy + 5 - 6 =$$
$$6xy^2 + 4xy - 1$$

29 B Here's how to crack it: Attack the answers. The correct answer will have two numbers that multiply together to get –18 (eliminating **C** and **D**) and ADD together to get –7 (eliminating **A**). It doesn't get much easier than that, eh?

Of course, you could always solve the problem the old-fashioned way. Break the equation, $x^2 - 7x - 18$, into two binomials:

$$(x - ?)(x + ?)$$

What numbers multiply together to be –18 and add together to be –7? Hopefully, –9 and 2 came to mind. That's it: $(x - 9)(x + 2)$.

30 J **Here's how to crack it:** No shortcuts here, you just have to factor:

$$\frac{x^2 - 2x - 15}{x^2 + x - 6} = \frac{(x-5)(x+3)}{(x-2)(x+3)} = \frac{x-5}{x-2}$$

31 B **Here's how to crack it:** Plug In, Plug In, Plug In! The correct answer should satisfy each set of ordered pairs. **A**, **C**, and **D** work for 1 or 2 of the ordered pairs, but only **B** works for all 4, making it the correct answer.

32 H **Here's how to crack it:** Figure out the pattern. In this case the pattern first adds 10, then multiplies by 2. When our pattern reaches the element in question, it's time to multiply by 2, making our correct answer 78 • 2, or 156.

33 A **Here's how to crack it:** Again, Plug In. Only **A** satisfies all the ordered pairs. For example, we'll use the second column of the chart to verify a right and wrong answer:

$$A: i = 1,000(i) + 500$$
$$i = 1000(l) + 500 = 1000(15) + 500$$
$$15,000 + 500 = 15,500$$

So answer choice **A** works.

Wrong answers won't work with every choice, like **D**:

$$i = 400(l) + 12,500 = 400(15) + 12,500 =$$
$$6,000 + 12,500 =$$
$$18,500$$

Since 15,500 does not equal 18,500, **D** is not the right answer.

34 G Here's how to crack it: Remember, domain goes in, range comes out. When we plug in −4, −2 and 1 into the function is spits out **G**.

$$\frac{-64+16-4}{2} = \frac{-52}{2} = -26$$

$$\frac{-8+4-2}{2} = \frac{-6}{2} = -3$$

$$\frac{1+1+1}{2} = \frac{3}{2}$$

35 C Here's how to crack it: Domain in, range out. So we have to attack our answer choices to see which domain spits out 22, 84, and 130. We can save ourselves a lot of work here. **D** goes immediately, and would only be selected by a student who has confused domain and range. From there we can check $f(-2)$ and find that it equals 18, *not* 22, meaning **C** is our only alternative (and the correct answer).

36 G Here's how to crack it: This is a tough question. Let's review. To find where a graph crosses the y-axis, we set the equation to 0, which will involve factoring, as so:

$$f(x) = x^3 - 2x^2 - 8x$$

$$x^3 - 2x^2 - 8x = 0$$

$$x(x^2 - 2x - 8) = 0$$

$$x(x-4)(x+2) = 0$$

$$x = 0, 4, -2$$

To find where on the graph a function crosses the y-axis, simply plug in 0 for x. In this case, setting x to 0 sets the entire equation to 0, meaning the y-intercept must be at 0. This question doesn't ask for the ordered pairs, only the points on the x- and y-axis that the graph crosses.

37 C Here's how to crack it: In this problem, where there's an x, there's an 8! Plug 8 into the function and compute accordingly:

$$f(8) = 8^2 - 16 + 5 = 64 - 11 = 53$$

38 J Here's how to crack it: This is essentially the same question as 36, except now you need to know the ordered pair(s) where the graph crosses the axis. It requires one extra step. First do the factoring. For x, set the equation equal to 0:

$$f(x) = x^2 - 6x + 9 = 0$$
$$(x-3)(x-3) = 0$$
$$x = 3$$

So the graph crosses the axis at 3, which would be (3, 0) on the coordinate plane. That eliminates **G** and **H**. Now, simply plug 0 in for x to find the y-intercept. That gives us +9, and an ordered pair of (0, 9) leaving only **J** as the correct answer.

39 A Here's how to crack it: The formula for indirect variation is $y = \dfrac{k}{x}$ where k is the constant. Memorize this. Also, in an indirect variation, as x increases, y decreases, so we know the number must get smaller. That's a big help, because only **A** is smaller than 14, so we can steal the answer to this question quickly. If we wanted to figure it out normally, we could plug our values into the formula for indirect variation, and we'd get $14 = \dfrac{k}{7}$. This makes $k = 98$. Plugging $x = 42$, we now get $y = \dfrac{98}{42}$, or $2\dfrac{1}{3}$.

40 H Here's how to crack it: Remember, in a function, the domain value will never repeat. Never. So **H** takes the cake, as it is the only domain that does not have a value that repeats.

41 B Here's how to crack it: Use the vertical line test. Notice that **B** fails this test miserably.

If you draw a vertical line on the graph, it intersects the line in graph **B** in two spots. This means **B** can't represent a function, since some domain values must repeat.

42 F Here's how to crack it: The formula for direct variation is $y = k(x)$, and you can pick any ordered pair for the chart to solve for the constant (k). Any point you pick should give you a constant of 500. For example, we'll pick the first values from the chart:

$$10,000(\$) = 20(\text{laws}) \bullet k$$

$$k = 500$$

Then we need to solve:

$$1,000,000 = 500x$$
$$2,000 = x$$

43 B Here's how to crack it: This problem should be easy. This is an elaborate way of asking you to take your initial matrix and multiply all of its values by 4. Do that, and you'll get B, the correct answer.

44 J Here's how to crack it: Add each corresponding value in the two matrices (i.e., 24 and 16, 19 and –5, etc.). **D** matches every sum correctly.

45 C Here's how to crack it: This question is a little more subtle. The question wants the inventory at pairs of pants at a particular clothing store. We start with 28 short and 49 tall pairs of pants, and then sold 17 and 32. We end up with 11 short and 17 tall, for a total of 28, or **C**.

46 J Here's how to crack it: A reminder: Mean is average; Median is middle; and mode is most (occurring). Let's start with the easiest value to calculate, the mode. 6.7 occurs twice, more than any other number making it the mode. So **B** and **C** are already out. Now let's list the numbers in order and find the median.

$$(4.8, 5.2, 6.7, 6.7, 8)$$

What falls in the middle? 6.7, our median. That makes **D** our correct answer without computing the average at all! In case you wanted to be sure that the average is correct, here is the calculation:

$$\frac{4.8 + 5.2 + 6.7 + 6.7 + 8}{5} = 6.28$$

47 D Here's how to crack it: Just don't pick **A**. Unlike addition, we don't combine the corresponding elements according to the operation (in this case multiplication).

Remember, you multiply the row of matrix (**A**) by the both columns of matrix (**B**)

As so:

Matrix (A) Matrix (B)

$$\begin{bmatrix} 8 & 3 \\ 6 & 4 \end{bmatrix} \cdot \begin{bmatrix} -2 & 5 \\ -7 & 1 \end{bmatrix} = \begin{bmatrix} -16 + -21 & 40 + 3 \\ -12 + -28 & 30 + 4 \end{bmatrix} = \begin{bmatrix} -37 & 43 \\ -40 & 34 \end{bmatrix}$$

48 G Here's how to crack it: Stem-and-Leaf charts look tough, but they're actually a breeze. The median will fall right in the middle. Just cross out high and low numbers until you've isolated the middle number, in this case 32.

Stem	Leaf
1	88899
2	0114689
3	112567
4	00126
5	00345

49 A Here's how to crack it: Two important, quick pieces of information can be gleaned from any box-and-whisker graph: **B** the high and low-numbers in a set and the median. This should be plenty to get the question correct. The stem-and-leaf chart indicates that 22 is our low number and 56 is our high. Only **A** and **C** reflect this in the box-and-whisker graph, so **B** and **D** are out.

Finally the stripe in the middle of each box should indicate the median. With a little analysis, we can isolate 34 and 36 as the two numbers that fall in the middle, making their average, 35, the median. Only **A** is close, and we're done with this question.

50 G Here's how to crack it: Backsolve. Your goal is to pick the line that cuts the points in half and most accurately traces the progression of the point in general. If this hurts your brain, then briefly sketch the lines described in the answers. **F** and **J** want to give the line y-intercepts that are significantly far away from any of the points in the scatterplot and **H** gives a giant slope (+4) that would break radically from the progression of the point.

If there was any doubt, you could sketch **G** and find that its line cuts the points right in half. See the following graph:

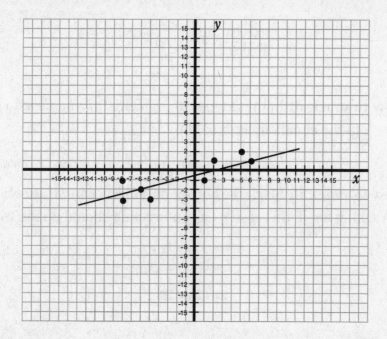

Note that **H** also cuts the points in half, but it does not run through two of our plotted points, AND it doesn't follow the general progression of the points.

51 C Here's how to crack it: Remember your formula for direct variation: $y = kx$.

From there we plug in and solve for *k*:

$$10 = (k)(7)$$
$$\frac{10}{7} = k$$

Now we can plug into the formula to solve for *y* when *x* is 10, since *k* is our constant of $\frac{10}{7}$.

$$y = \frac{10}{7}(10)$$
$$y = \frac{100}{7}$$
$$y = 14\frac{2}{7}$$

52 J Here's how to crack it: Plug into the formula!

$$c = \frac{100,000}{10,000}(1.5) + 11.00 = 15 + 11 = 26$$

53 C Here's how to crack it: In these types of problems, all you have to do is put the given figure into the equation, like so: $f(5) = 5^3 + 5 - 7 = 130 - 7 = 123$

54 G Here's how to crack it: Stack the equations and pay careful attention to what the question is asking for, in this case $x + y$. Subtracting should do the trick nicely:

$$\begin{array}{r} 4x + 7y = 12 \\ -(2x + 5y = -10) \\ \hline 2x + 2y = 22 \end{array}$$

From here we can use the distributive property to solve for $x + y$:

$$2x + 2y = 22$$
$$2(x + y) = 22$$
$$(x + y) = 11$$

55 B Here's how to crack it: Pay attention to the answer choices! You want the range for t, and the question gives you the form of:

$$225 > 3t > 246$$

So, we need to divide the entire equation through by 3, as so:

$$\frac{225}{3} > \frac{3t}{3} > \frac{246}{3}$$
$$75 > t > 82$$

56 G Here's how to crack it: Backsolve or use Algebra, it's really up to you. If Mary was 100 pounds, John would weigh 200 pounds, making the difference 100 pounds. That's wrong. If Mary weighed 200 pounds, John would be 400 pounds, making the difference 200 pounds, just as the problem specified. So Backsolving is certainly the easiest way.

Here's the algebra, just in case:

$j = 2m$, and $j - m = 200$ These are simultaneous equations, so let's solve for j:

$j - m = 200$ So, by adding m to both sides we get:

$j = 200 + m$ Now we can substitute j for $2m$ (since $j = 2m$):

$2m = 200 + m$ By subtracting m from both sides we get the answer:

$m = 200$

57 D Here's how to crack it: Backsolve! Notice only 3 will plug into the slope formula to give us a slope of $-\dfrac{2}{5}$:

$$\frac{x_2 - x_1}{y_2 - y_1} = \text{slope}$$

$$\frac{z(3) - 5}{3 - -2} = \frac{3 - 5}{5} = -\frac{2}{5}$$

58 G Here's how to crack it: Don't forget POE! You have a positive (tilting upward, moving from left to right) slope and a negative (tilting downward from left to right) slope, so there product must be negative. **H** and **J** are gone. Further scrutiny reveals −3 and 1 as our two slopes, giving us a product of −3.

59 C Here's how to crack it: Plug in from the figures they give you, as follows:

$$x^2 + 2xy + y^2$$
$$4^2 + 2(4)(-3) + (-3)^2 =$$
$$16 + -24 + 9 = 1$$

60 F Here's how to crack it: This problem is a little tricky, eh? Remember, 2 should go into the function, and 7 should come out. Plugging 2 into the four equations in the answer choices, we get **F** = 7, **G** = 6, **H** = 16, and **J** = 6. So **F** is the answer. Here's how **F** works:

$$x^3 - 1$$
$$2^3 - 1 = 7$$
$$8 - 1 = 7$$
$$7 = 7$$
right!

Chapter 10

Practice Test 2

Note: On the actual End-of-Course Algebra I SOL exam, you may see a weird negative symbol. Instead of the usual -7, you will probably see a $^-7$. Minus signs will stil look the same, such as $5x - 3y - 9$. But negative numbers will look like $^-9$. Don't let it fool you.

1 Solve the following linear equation for x:

$$5x + 13 = 43$$

A −6

B −3

C 0

D 6

2 Apples are sold to a store in Yorktown based on the following formula:

$$p = 4a + 14 - y$$

Where a is the number of pounds of apples purchased and y is the "Yorktown Discount." How much must this store pay if they want 1,000 pounds of apples and the "Yorktown Discount" is $30?

F $3,956

G $3,984

H $4,014

J $4,044

3 The temperature in the month of July in Thailand always satisfies the following condition:

$$269 < 3t + 5 < 320$$

Which inequality properly expresses this condition?

A $88 < t < 105$

B $93 < t < 110$

C $99 < t < 115$

D $104 < t < 120$

4 Given that $a = b$, which of the following is equal to $b - c$?

F $\dfrac{a}{b}$

G $a - b$

H $a - c$

J $c - a$

5 If $a = c$ and $b = 12$, which of the following statements would justify the conclusion that a also equals 12?

A $c + a = 26$

B $c = b - 1$

C $b + a = c + a$

D $c - a = b$

6 Which of the following is the graph of a line with a y-intercept of 5 and a slope of –3?

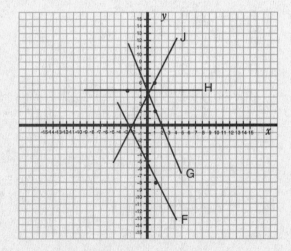

7 Points $(x, 7)$ and $(-5, 12)$ lie on the same line and have a slope of $\frac{1}{2}$. Which of the following answer choices represents x?

A –25

B –20

C 20

D 25

8 What is the slope of the following graph?

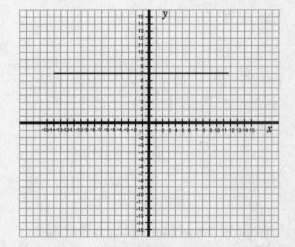

F Undefined

G 0

H 1

J Infinite

9 What is the slope of the line in the following graph?

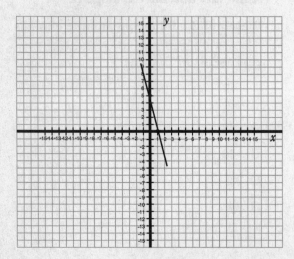

A –5

B –4

C 4

D 5

10 What is the y-intercept of a line that has a x-intercept of 5 and a slope of 3?

F –30

G –20

H –15

J 15

11 What is the equation of a line that contains points (–20, –5) and (10, 10)?

A $y = \dfrac{x}{4}$

B $y = x$

C $y = +5$

D $y = \dfrac{x}{2} - 5$

12 What is the solution to this system of equations?

$$\begin{cases} 7 - x = y + 3 \\ 3y - x = 12 \end{cases}$$

F $x = 4, y = 0$

G $x = 3, y = 1$

H $x = 3, y = 3$

J $x = 0, y = 4$

13 What is the solution to this system of equations?

$$\begin{cases} \dfrac{y}{3} + x = -2 \\ 2x + y = -8 \end{cases}$$

A $x = -4, y = 6$

B $x = 0, y = -6$

C $x = 2, y = 0$

D $x = 2, y = -12$

14 A man bought two tickets and one hot dog at the circus. His total was $18.50. Another woman bought four tickets and one hot dog. Her total was $37.00. What was the price of one ticket and one hot dog?

F $10.00

G $11.00

H $11.50

J $12.00

15 How many solutions does the following system of equations have?

$$\begin{cases} 8x + 6y = 20 \\ 16x + 12y = 40 \end{cases}$$

A 0

B 1

C 2

D Infinite

16 Which of the following would represent the equations of the following graph?

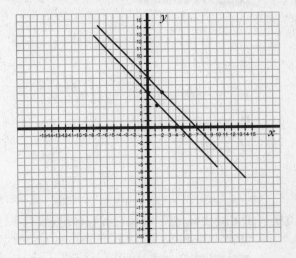

F $8x + 4y = 20$

   $8x + 4y = 28$

G $y - 2x = 5$

   $y + 2x = 7$

H $4x + 2y = 17$

   $4x + 2y = 10$

J $y - 2x = 7$

   $y - 2x = 14$

17 What are the solutions to the following equation?

$$\{x^2 - 3x - 18 = 0\}$$

A $x = -3, -6$

B $x = -3, 6$

C $x = 3, -6$

D $x = 3, 6$

18 What are the x-intercepts of the parabola that the following quadratic equation creates?

$$x^2 - 25 = 0$$

F $x = -5$

G $x = -5$ or -10

H $x = 5$ or -5

J $x = 25$

19 If the distance between two stars is approximately $5.5 \cdot 10^{18}$ miles, about how many years would it take a spaceship traveling at $1.5 \cdot 10^3$ miles per year to get from one star to the other?

A $3.6\overline{6} \cdot 10^{15}$

B $3.6\overline{6} \cdot 10^6$

C $36.\overline{6} \cdot 10^4$

D $366 \cdot 10^3$

20 If a car travels approximately $4.2 \cdot 10^5$ inches in one hour, how many inches does the car travel in 300 hours?

F $.126 \cdot 10^5$

G $1.26 \cdot 10^6$

H $12.6 \cdot 10^7$

J $126 \cdot 10^8$

21 If you round $\sqrt{24}$ and $\sqrt{45}$ to the nearest tenth, what is their sum?

A 11.5

B 11.6

C 11.7

D 11.8

22 What is the value of $4x - 7 + x^2y$ if $x = 3$ and $y = -4$?

F -31

G 31

H 36

J 50

23 What is the value of $\dfrac{4x^2 + 5y - 1}{xy + 3}$, if $x = -4$ and $y = 1$?

A 68

B 0

C -68

D -80

24 Every time Vince takes a trip, he travels twice as far the first day as he travels on the second day. On Vince's current trip, he arrived at his destination on the second day. If he travels 25 miles on the second day, how many miles was his total trip?

F 25 miles

G 50 miles

H 75 miles

J 100 miles

25 If $\dfrac{2}{3}$ of x is equal to 24, what is x?

A 9

B 18

C 36

D 72

26 If $a = (3y + 5)$ and $b = (4x - y)$, what is ab?

F $3y^2 - 5y + 20x$

G $12xy + 20x - 5y$

H $12xy - 3y^2 + 20x - 5y$

J $2y + 9x - 5y + 20$

27 If $c = (x + y)$ and $d = (x - y)$, what is $c \bullet d$?

A $x^2 - y^2$

B 0

C 1

D $2x - 2y$

28 Which of the following is equivalent to $\dfrac{6x + 24}{12}$?

F $\dfrac{1}{2}x + 2x^2$

G $x + 2$

H $\dfrac{x + 4}{2}$

J $\dfrac{x + 2}{6}$

29 What is the value of $\dfrac{5xy^2 + xy + 14x}{5y^2 + y + 14}$

if $x = 12$ and $y = -40$?

A −480

B −12

C 12

D 480

30 Simplify the following expression:

$$\dfrac{x^2 - y^2}{x^2 + 2xy + y^2}$$

F $\dfrac{1}{2xy}$

G $\dfrac{x^2}{y^2}$

H $\dfrac{x - y}{x + y}$

J $\dfrac{x + y}{x - y}$

31 The following is the list of a domain and range from a certain function. Which of the following equations could represent the algebraic operation this function performs?

Domain (x)	2	3	4	5	6	7
Range (y)	6	12	20	30	42	56

A $y = x^2 + 2$

B $y = x^2 + 3$

C $y = x^2 + 5$

D $y = x^2 + x$

32 Which of the following represents the omitted term in the following pattern?

10, 5, 15, 10, 30, 25, ___, 70, 210 . .

F 30

G 50

H 75

J 205

33 The following is the list of a domain and range from a certain function. Which of the following equations could represent the algebraic operation this function performs?

Domain (x)	3	6	9	12	15	18
Range (y)	$\dfrac{2}{3}$	$\dfrac{4}{3}$	2	$\dfrac{8}{3}$	$\dfrac{10}{3}$	4

A $y = \dfrac{2}{x}$

B $y = \dfrac{8}{x}$

C $y = \dfrac{\frac{x}{3} + x}{6}$

D $y = \dfrac{18}{x}$

34 What is the range of the function $f(x) = x^2 + 9x + 24$ when the domain is $\{-3, 6, 7\}$?

F $\{-6, 114, 136\}$

G $\{-6, 94, 136\}$

H $\{6, 114, 136\}$

J $\{6, 25, 49\}$

35 What is the domain of function $f(x) = \dfrac{3x^2}{2x}$, if the range is $\{-3, 9, 12\}$?

A $\left\{\dfrac{27}{6}, 13.5, 18\right\}$

B $\{-2, -6, 8\}$

C $\{2, 6, 8\}$

D $\{-2, 6, 8\}$

36 If $f(x) = \dfrac{x^2 + x + 3}{6}$, then what is the value of $f(5)$?

F 33

G $\dfrac{33}{6}$

H 16

J $\dfrac{16}{6}$

37 At what points does the graph of this function intersect the x- and y-axes?

$$f(x) = x^2 + 5x - 24$$

A x: $(x = 3, 0)$; y: $(y = 9, 24)$

B x: $(x = 0, -8)$ and $(0, -3)$; y: $(y = 0, -24)$

C x: $(x = 8, 0)$ and $(3, 0)$; y: $(y = 0, -24)$

D x: $(x = -8, 0)$ and $(3, 0)$; y: $(y = 0, -24)$

38 At what x- and y-coordinates does this function cross the x- and y-axes?

$$f(x) = x^3 - 16x$$

  F x: $\{x = 0, -4, 4\}$; y: $\{y = 0\}$

  G x: $\{x = 0, 4\}$; y: $\{y = -16\}$

  H x: $\{x = 0, -4\}$; y: $\{y = -16\}$

  J x: $\{x = 0\}$; y: $\{y = 0, 16\}$

39 If y varies directly with x, and y is 45 when x is 36; what is y when x is 60?

  A 48

  B 75

  C 108

  D 216

40 Of the following sets of ordered pairs, expressed as domain (x) and range (y) which set does NOT represent a function?

  F Domain $\{-1, 5, 7, 12\}$

       Range $\{1, 25, 79, 144\}$

  G Domain $\{2, 4, 6, 8\}$

       Range $\{5, 9, 13, 17\}$

  H Domain $\{-1, 1, -2, 2\}$

       Range $\{2, 5\}$

  J Domain $\{2, 2, 3, 4, 4, 5\}$

       Range $\{2, 4, 6, 8, 10, 12\}$

41 Which of the following graphs represents a function?

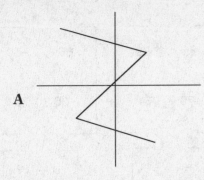

A

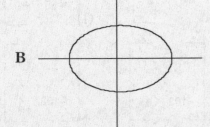

B

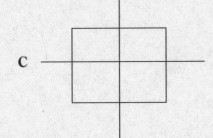

C

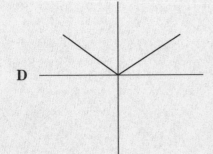

D

42 The following chart relates the total tax bill per person (*t*) to the total number of residents who live in Ocean Beach (*ob*).

Total Tax Bill (*t*)	Residents of Ocean Beach (*ob*)
$100	5,000
$66.67	7,500
$50	10,000
$40	12,500

If (*t*) continues to vary indirectly with (*ob*), what would each person's tax bill be if there were 15,000 residents of Ocean Beach?

F $45

G $36.67

H $33.33

J $30

43 The following matrix represents the sales total of two pet store owners at their respective shops:

	Ralph	Doug
Iguanas	25	14
Rats	17	13
Parakeets	33	11

If each pet store owner must pay the government a 150% tax for each sale he makes, which of the following matrices represents the tax each owner must pay?

A
Ralph	Doug
$37.50	$21.00
$25.50	$19.50
$49.50	$16.50

B
Ralph	Doug
$37.50	$21.00
$30.00	$20.00
$49.50	$16.50

C
Ralph	Doug
$37.50	$21.00
$25.50	$19.50
$50.00	$17.00

D
Ralph	Doug
$40.00	$20.00
$25.50	$19.50
$49.50	$16.50

44 What is the difference between the two following matrices?

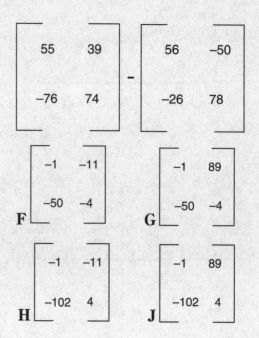

$$\begin{bmatrix} 55 & 39 \\ -76 & 74 \end{bmatrix} - \begin{bmatrix} 56 & -50 \\ -26 & 78 \end{bmatrix}$$

F
$$\begin{bmatrix} -1 & -11 \\ -50 & -4 \end{bmatrix}$$

G
$$\begin{bmatrix} -1 & 89 \\ -50 & -4 \end{bmatrix}$$

H
$$\begin{bmatrix} -1 & -11 \\ -102 & 4 \end{bmatrix}$$

J
$$\begin{bmatrix} -1 & 89 \\ -102 & 4 \end{bmatrix}$$

45 The following two matrices represent the stock and sales of a certain companies' goo-goo doll collection for the Month of May, 1999:

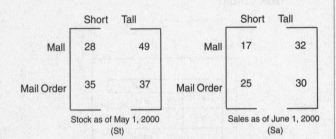

Stock as of May 1, 2000 (St)

Sales as of June 1, 2000 (Sa)

How many short goo-goo dolls are available through mail-order?

A   7

B   9

C   10

D   11

46 Which of the following sets represents the mean, median, and mode, respectively for the following set of data?

Data: {11, 13, 15, 16, 16, 23}

F {15.67, 15, 16}

G {15.67 15.5, 16}

H {15.67, 17, 23}

J {15.7, 17, 15}

47 Which of the following represents the product of the following two matrices?

$$\begin{bmatrix} -5 & 5 \\ -4 & 7 \end{bmatrix} \quad \begin{bmatrix} 3 & -3 \\ 6 & 2 \end{bmatrix}$$

A $\begin{bmatrix} -15 & -15 \\ -24 & -14 \end{bmatrix}$ B $\begin{bmatrix} -45 & 45 \\ -36 & -7 \end{bmatrix}$

C $\begin{bmatrix} 15 & 25 \\ 30 & 26 \end{bmatrix}$ D $\begin{bmatrix} 56 & 42 \\ 38 & 41 \end{bmatrix}$

48 The following stem-and-leaf chart shows the results of the state lottery in the past five drawings. What is the mode of the numbers selected in the drawing?

Stem	Leaf
0	234
1	24667
2	000056789
3	12
4	00345

F 12

G 20

H 32

J 45

49 The following Stem-and-Leaf Chart represents the number of hours a week a group of selected 8th graders spend online. Which of the following Box-and-Whisker graphs best represents this chart?

Stem	Leaf
6	234
7	24667
8	56789
9	12

A

B

C

D

232

CRACKING THE VIRGINIA SOL: EOC ALGEBRA I

50 Using the Median-Fit method, which equation most likely represents the line of best fit for the data shown in the scatterplot?

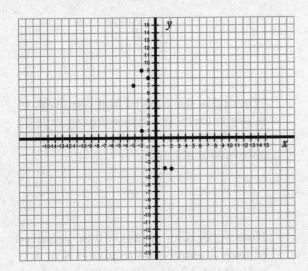

F $y = -\dfrac{7}{3x}$

G $y = -\dfrac{7x}{3} + 4$

H $y = -\dfrac{x}{2}$

J $y = \dfrac{x}{2-5}$

51 The following chart represents the population of Southland High by age:

Age	# of Kids
13	20
14	30
15	30
16	40

What is the sum of the median and the mode of the group?

A 20

B 30

C 31

D 40

52 What is the range of the function

$$f(x) = \frac{x^2 + 13}{x - 3}$$

for the domain {5, 9, 13}

F (19, 15.67, 18.2)

G (19, –52, –91)

H (–10, –15, –20)

J (all positive numbers)

53 What is $(x + y)(x - y)$ if $x = 7$ and $y = -3$?

    A –4

    B 10

    C 21

    D 40

54 If y varies indirectly with x, and $x = 4$ while $y = 12$, what is the value of x when $y = 6$?

    F 2

    G 4

    H 6

    J 8

55 The amount of fuel required to reach Planet X is determined by the following formula:

$$f = \frac{\frac{v}{.2} \bullet A}{2}$$

Where f is the tons of fuel required, v is the velocity the spaceship in miles per minute, and a is the number of astronauts aboard.

How many tons of fuel will be required to take 5 astronauts to planet X at a velocity of 1000 miles per minute?

    A 10,000

    B 12,500

    C 15,000

    D 30,000

56 What are the x-intercepts of the parabola created by the function $f(x) = x^2 - 169$?

    F $x = 0$

    G $x = 13$

    H $x = 13$ and -13

    J $x = -13$

57 Where does the following function cross both the x– and y–axes?

$f(x) = x^2 + 5x - 14$

A $x = -7, 2$ $y = -14$

B $x = 7, 2$ $y = 14$

C $x = 7$ $y = 0$

D $x = 2$ $y = 7$

58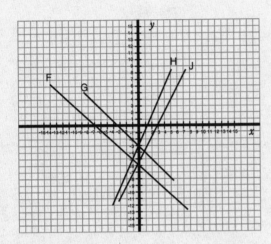

Which of the following lines above represents the equation: $2y - 4x = -6$

59 What is the value of $3x^2 - 5xy + y^2$, if $x = 3$ and $y = -4$?

A -20

B -25

C 103

D 250

60 If $f(3) = -1$, which of the following equations could represent $f(x)$?

F $x^3 - 12$

G $x^3 - 2$

H $x^2 + 2$

J $x^2 - 10$

Chapter 11

Practice Test 2 Answers and Explanations

Answer Key

1 **D**
2 **G**
3 **A**
4 **H**
5 **C**
6 **G**
7 **A**
8 **G**
9 **A**
10 **H**
11 **C**
12 **J**
13 **D**
14 **F**
15 **D**
16 **F**
17 **B**
18 **H**
19 **A**
20 **H**
21 **B**
22 **F**
23 **C**
24 **H**
25 **C**
26 **H**
27 **A**
28 **H**
29 **C**
30 **H**

1 D Here's how to crack it: Isolate the variable, then solve for x:

$$5x + 13 = 43$$

$$5x + 13 - 13 = 43 - 13$$

$$5x = 30$$

$$x = 6$$

2 G Here's how to crack it: Plug into the formula with the numbers given:

$$p = 4\,(1000) + 14 - 30 = 3984$$

3 A Here's how to crack it: Subtract 5 from all sides of the inequality and then solve.

$$269 < 3t + 5 < 320$$
$$\frac{-5 \qquad -5 \qquad -5}{269 - 5 < 3t + 5 - 5 < 320 - 5}$$
$$264 < 3t < 315$$
$$\frac{264}{3} < \frac{3t}{3} < \frac{315}{3}$$
$$88 < t < 105$$

4 H Here's how to crack it: Plug In all the way. If you make $a = 3$, $b = 3$, and $c = 4$ you could quickly eliminate all answers but **H**. (This is an example of the Substitution Property, by the way.)

5 C Here's how to crack it: This problem is similar to #4, with some extra wording. Remember the Transitive Property. Plug In if there's any confusion.

6 G **Here's how to crack it:** Attack the answers! **F** is quickly eliminated because its *y*-intercept is not 5, and **H** is gone because its slope is 0. That leaves only **G** and **J**, and only **G** has the negative slope we're looking for. No calculation is needed whatsoever!

7 A **Here's how to crack it:** Know the slope formula by heart!

From here we can cross-multiply the fractions, which means we'd multiply the 5 times the 4, and the (–5 –*x*) by 1 to give us:

$$-5 - x = 20$$

$$\underline{+5 \qquad +5}$$

$$-x = 25$$

$$x = -25 \text{ or } \mathbf{A}$$

$$\frac{rise}{run} = \frac{y_2 - y_1}{x_2 - x_1}$$

$$\frac{rise}{run} = \frac{12 - 7}{-5 - x} = \frac{1}{4} =$$

$$\frac{5}{-5 - x} = \frac{5}{-5 - (-25)} = \frac{5}{-5 + 25} = \frac{5}{20} = \frac{1}{4}$$

8 G **Here's how to crack it:** A straight line does not increase vertically as *x* increases horizontally, so it has a slope of 0. A straight vertical line's slope is undefined.

9 A **Here's how to crack it:** At this point you should recognize the slope is negative and immediately cross out **C** and **D**. In this line, *y* drops 5 as *x* increases by 1, so **A** is the correct answer.

31	D
32	H
33	C
34	H
35	D
36	G
37	D
38	F
39	B
40	J
41	D
42	H
43	A
44	G
45	C
46	G
47	C
48	G
49	D
50	F
51	C
52	F
53	D
54	J
55	B
56	H
57	A
58	H
59	C
60	J

10 H Here's how to crack it: Memorize the equation of a line and plug in. At the x-intercept, y will be 0, so we can make an equation that looks like this:

$$b = -15$$

$$mx + b = 0$$

$$3(5) + b \text{ (our } y\text{-intercept)} = 0$$

$$\frac{15 + b = 0}{\underset{-15\qquad -15}{b = -15}}$$

11 C Here's how to crack it: Backsolve the equations into the points. Only with the right equation will both x and y fit. **A** works for the first ordered pair, and **B** works for the second. Only **C** plugs in correctly for both.

$$-5 = -5$$
$$-5 = \frac{1}{2}(-20) + 5$$

$$5 = 5$$
$$10 = \frac{1}{2}(10) + 5$$

12 J Here's how to crack it: Backsolve. Only **J** works for both equations.

$$7 - x = y + 3$$

$$7 - 0 = 4 + 3$$

$$7 = 7$$

$$3y - x = 12$$

$$3(4) - 0 = 12$$

$$12 - 0 = 12$$

We're going to show you how to solve this problem with algebra, but we recommend Backsolving when it's possible. Rewrite the two equations as so:

Now, we can add the two equations:

$$\begin{Bmatrix} 7 - x = y + 3 \\ 3y - x = 12 \end{Bmatrix} = \begin{Bmatrix} x + y = 4 \\ -x + 3y = 12 \end{Bmatrix}$$

$$y = 4$$
$$x + y = 4$$
$$\underline{(+) -x + 3y = 12}$$
$$4y = 16$$

With $y = 0$, we know that x must equal 4, since we found that $x + y = 4$.

The answer is $x = 0$, $y = 4$, or answer choice **J**.

13 D Here's how to crack it: Backsolve again. Only D works for both equations.

$$\begin{cases} \dfrac{y}{3} + x = -2 \\ 2x + y = -8 \end{cases}$$

Answer **D** says y should be -12 and x should be 2, so let's check:

$$\begin{cases} \dfrac{-12}{3} + 2 = -2 \\ 2(2) + -12 = -8 \end{cases}$$

Right on!

14 F Here's how to crack it: We just ran out of shortcuts. Translate the English into equations and solve, either by substitution or addition/subtraction.

2 tickets plus 1 hot dog is $18.50:

$$2t + 1h = 18.50$$

4 tickets plus 1 hot dog is $37.00:

$$4t + 1h = 35.50$$

Here, we should stack the equations, and then subtract them to get rid of h and solve for a single ticket price:

$$\begin{aligned} 4t + h &= 35.50 \\ -\,(2t + h &= 18.50) \\ \hline 4t - 2t + h - h &= 35.50 - 18.50 \\ 2t &= 17 \\ t &= 8.50 \end{aligned}$$

Now we can substitute this value back in and solve for the hot dog:

$$2(8.5) + h = 18.50$$
$$17 + h = 18.50$$
$$h = 1.50$$

So, a ticket (8.50) plus a hot dog (1.50) would be $10, or **F**.

15 D Here's how to crack it: This question is kind of a curveball. Divide the second equation through by 2 and what do you have? The same equation as the top equation! They are actually the same equation, so any point you can substitute for one you could substitute in for the other. There are an infinite number of solutions.

16 F Here's how to crack it: Remember, parallel lines will be identical equations except for the y-intercept. That quickly eliminates **G**, because the equations are different, as well as their y-intercepts. From there you'll need to simplify each equation to check them against the given lines. When we divide **F** through by 4 (the lowest common denominator of all the coefficients), we get the following equations:

$$2x + y = 5$$

$$2x + y = 7$$

or

$$y = -2x + 5$$

$$y = -2x + 7$$

This gives us the y-intercepts that we're looking for as well as the exact negative slope drawn on the graph. Notice that **H** and **J** can be quickly eliminated, because their y-intercepts are not equivalent the graph's y-intercepts of 5 and 7.

17 B Here's how to crack it: Backsolve. Only **B** equates for both parts of the equation:

$$\{x^2 - 3x - 18 = 0\}$$
$$B = (-3,)$$
$$-3^2 - 3(-3) - 18 = 0$$
$$9 + 9 - 18 = 0$$

$$\{x^2 - 3x - 18 = 0\}$$
$$B = (+6)$$
$$-6^2 - 3(6) - 18 = 0$$
$$36 - 18 - 18 = 0$$

18 H Here's how to crack it: Try to identify the difference between two squares when it comes up. This ability can quickly lead you to a right answer. Does the following look familiar?

$$(x + y)(x - y)$$

Now apply it to this problem:

$$x^2 - 25 = 0$$
$$(x + 5)(x - 5) = 0$$
$$x = 5, -5$$

19 A Here's how to crack it: Here we need to divide using scientific notation. This will test your knowledge of exponent rules. Know them by heart. When dividing exponents of like base, you subtract like so:

$$\frac{5.5 \cdot 10^{18}}{1.5 \cdot 10^3} = 3.6\overline{6} \cdot 10^{15}$$

20 H Here's how to crack it: This problem is a little tricky, because we need to convert 300 into scientific notation before we can multiply. $300 = 3.0 \cdot 10^2$ which, when multiplied by $4.2 \cdot 10^5$ gives our $12.6 \cdot 10^7$, or **H**. The correct solution could also be written as $1.26 \cdot 10^8$, which was not an answer choice.

21 B Here's how to crack it: Calculator city. The square root of 24 is about 4.9 and the square root of 45 is about 6.7 (both rounded). The sum (addition) would be 11.6.

22 F Here's how to crack it: Plug In and avoid careless errors. $x = 3$, $y = -4$

$$4x - 7 + x^2 y$$

$$4(3) - 7 + (9)(-4) =$$

$$12 - 7 - 36 = -31$$

23 C Here's how to crack it: Plug and Chug:

$$\frac{4(-4)^2 + 5(1) - 1}{-4(1) + 3} = \frac{4(16) + 4}{-4 + 3} = \frac{68}{-1} = -68$$

24 H Here's how to crack it: If Vince traveled 25 miles the second day, the question says he would have traveled twice as much on the first day—50 miles. So by the end of the second day, add the miles together for the total of 75, or **H**

25 C Here's how to crack it: Translate the English into an equation and solve.

$$\frac{2x}{3} = 24$$

To isolate the x from $\frac{2x}{3}$, multiply the fraction by its inverse, $\frac{3}{2}$. And, of course, whatever you do to one side, you do to the other.

$$\left(\frac{3}{2}\right)\frac{2}{3x} = 24\left(\frac{3}{2}\right) x = 36$$

26 H Here's how to crack it: FOIL. Know FOIL like it's your best friend.

$$(3y + 5)(4x - y) = 12xy \text{ (first)} - 3y^2 \text{ (outer)} + 20x \text{ (inner)} - 5y \text{ (last)}$$

27 A Here's how to crack it: This is the difference of squares again. It saves time if you can recognize it, but you could always FOIL the binomials if you weren't sure. Refer to chapter 3 if you need refreshing.

28 H Here's how to crack it: You could factor or Plug In. The easiest thing to do is notice that every number in the equation is divisible by six. Divided by 6,

$\dfrac{6x+24}{12}$ reduces to $\dfrac{x+4}{2}$.

If you wanted to Plug In, set x is equal to an integer, such as 4. Then $\dfrac{6x+24}{12}$ becomes $\dfrac{48}{12}$, or our target number of 4. Only **H** gives us this target when we plug 4 in for x.

29 C Here's how to crack it: You could just plug in the values given, but factoring can save you significant computational time. Notice that x is common to all three terms on the top equation. This can be factored as so:

$$\frac{5xy^2 + xy + 14x}{5y^2 + y + 14} = \frac{x(5y^2 + y + 14)}{5y^2 + y + 14} = x$$

Pretty cool, huh? Factoring out x on the top part of the fraction left the exact same equation on the top and bottom, meaning they cancel out. We're left with only x, or 12 as our answer.

30 H Here's how to crack it: Memorize your common FOIL identities.

$$\frac{x^2 - y^2}{x^2 + 2xy + y^2} = \frac{(x+y)(x-y)}{(x+y)(x+y)} = \frac{x-y}{x+y}$$

31 D Here's how to crack it: Keep Plugging In ordered pairs until you find the function that works for all the pairs. Only **D** does this for every point. The tricky equations only work for some of the ordered pairs.

32 H Here's how to crack it: The pattern is subtractng 5 then multiplying by 3. The term in question needs to have 25 multiplied by 3, giving us 75.

33 C **Here's how to crack it:** Plug and chug. Only **C** works for all the points.

Domain (x)	3	6	9	12	15	18
Range (y)	$\dfrac{2}{3}$	$\dfrac{4}{3}$	2	$\dfrac{8}{3}$	$\dfrac{10}{3}$	4

For example, we'll pick the first domain and range value in the chart above. Notice how they both plug successfully into the equation:

$$y = \frac{\dfrac{x}{3} + x}{6}$$

$$y = \frac{\dfrac{3}{3} + 3}{6} = \frac{4}{6} = \frac{2}{3}$$

No other equation solves successfully for the domain and range of this function.

34 H **Here's how to crack it:** Domain goes into a function, range comes out. When we plug −3 into the function, we get +6, which eliminates **F** and **G**. When we plug 6 into the function, we get 114, eliminating **J**. Only **H** contains the ranges that $f(x) = x^2 + 9x + 24$ gives when the domains of −3, 6, and 7 are inputted.

35 D **Here's how to crack it:** The question here asks what domain will produce the given range. We have to Backsolve here. Answer choice **A** is distracting only if you confuse domain and range. Only **D** produces our desired range.

36 G **Here's how to crack it:** Plug in 5 for x!

$$f(5) = \frac{5^2 + 5 + 3}{6} = \frac{25 + 5 + 3}{6} = \frac{33}{6} \quad \text{or } \mathbf{G}. \text{ Not too tough, huh?}$$

37 D Here's how to crack it: This question is asking for the coordinates of the x- and y-intercepts. So we set the equation to 0 to solve for the x-intercepts.

We can quickly eliminate **B**, because none the choices its x-coordinate is 0. By definition, points at the x-intercept must be (number, 0). Points at the y-intercept must be (0, number), so we can cross out **A** for the same reason.

Here's the factoring:

$$x = -8, 3$$
$$0 = x^2 + 5x - 24$$
$$0 = (x+8)(x-3)$$

So the graph would cross the x-axis at (–8, 0) and (3, 0). Since **D** is the only answer choice that offers this option, it must be our answer.

38 F Here's how to crack it: To find the y-intercept, plug 0 in for x, and solve. This turns out to be quite a shortcut, because, $f(0) = 0$, and only 0, so the answer must be **F**. Set the equation equal to zero to verify our answer:

$$x = 0, -4, 4$$
$$0 = x^3 - 16x$$
$$x(x^2 - 16) = 0$$
$$x(x+4)(x-4) = 0$$

Again, we know the x-intercept is 0, 4, and –4, so we know that **F** must be correct.

39 B Here's how to crack it: Know the formula: $y = (k)x$, this gives us our constant of

Now plug in for $x = 60$:

$$y = \frac{45}{36}(60) \text{ or } \mathbf{B}.$$
$$y = 75$$

40 J Here's how to crack it: No element in the domain of a function may repeat. This rule is shamelessly violated by answer choice **J**, making it the right answer.

41 D Here's how to crack it: Apply the vertical line test to all four graphs. Only **D** passes.

Note that wherever you draw the line, there will be only one point of intersection, the crux of the vertical line test.

42 H Here's how to crack it: We can tell immediately that an indirect variation is involved, since t gets smaller as r gets bigger. **F** must be wrong, since t gets larger while the r gets bigger. From there, we plug into the formula and solve for the constant.

$$k = 500,000$$
$$y = \frac{k}{x}$$
$$100 = \frac{k}{5,000}$$

With our constant of 500,000, we can solve for our specific task, which is to find the amount of taxes each citizen would pay if there were 15,000 people in the town.

$\frac{500,000}{15,000}$ = 33.33 repeating, rounded to $33.33.

43 A Here's how to crack it: Each value in the matrix need to be multiplied by 150%, or 1.5. Only **A** gives us all the correct products in the correct places.

44 G Here's how to crack it: Subtraction/Addition of Matrices is breeze. In this case, subtract the corresponding values from the two matrices and you'll get **G**. Remember, when you subtract a negative number, you add its opposite (or inverse). That's the only trap the wrong answer choices have laid in this question.

45 C Here's how to crack it: Just read the matrix! We started with 35 short Mail Order goo-goo dolls, then sold 25 of them. That leaves us with 10, or **C**.

46 G Here's how to crack it: When asked to find the mean, the median, and the mode from a set of numbers, start with the mode, or most occurring, because it's the easiest (or "most easy.") 16 occurs twice, the other elements only once, meaning **H** and **J** must go. The test listed the numbers in order, and we can see that 15 and 16 fall directly in the middle. The median must be the average of the two numbers, which is 15.5. Again, we don't even have to compute the average—**G** has it.

47 C Here's how to crack it: Don't pick **A**! Remember, matrix multiplication involves row times column!

$$\text{Matrix (A)} \quad \text{Matrix (B)}$$

$$\begin{bmatrix} -5 & 5 \\ -4 & 7 \end{bmatrix} \cdot \begin{bmatrix} 3 & -3 \\ 6 & 2 \end{bmatrix} = \begin{bmatrix} -15 + 30 & 15 + 10 \\ -12 + 42 & 12 + 14 \end{bmatrix}$$

The correct answer is $\begin{bmatrix} 15 & 25 \\ 30 & 26 \end{bmatrix}$ or **C**.

48 G Here's how to crack it: Mode means most occurring, and 20 occurs 4 times in this stem-and-leaf chart. It is the only number to repeat that often, so it's **B**.

49 D Here's how to crack it: Start with high and low numbers from the stem and leaf chart. The low number is 62, the high number is 92. Only **C** and **D** reflect this. Then flush out the median, which is 77 in the above chart.

Stem	Leaf
6	234
7	24667
8	56789
9	12

Only **D** is anywhere close to our median of 77, and it's the right answer.

50 F Here's how to crack it: Backsolve. We hope you've noticed the theme of elimination to our recommendations on these questions. The points tend to be in a negative slope, so **J** is out immediately. From there, sketch the three remaining lines and see which cut the points in half. Both **F** and **H** do, but **G** does not, so it's out. From there just ask yourself which line follows the points most closely, and we hope you'll agree it's **F**, the correct answer.

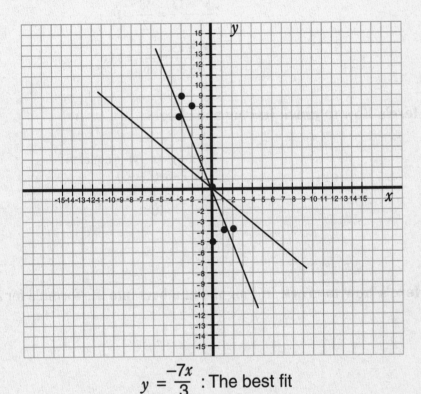

$$y = \frac{-7x}{3} : \text{The best fit}$$

51 C Here's how to crack it: Remember that finding a sum requires addition, so now we just need to determine the median and mode of the chart. The median is the value that would land in the middle if the numbers were listed in order. There are 120 ages listed on the chart here, so the 60th child will have the median age. We have only 13, 14, 15 and 16 year olds that are listed, and the 60th child must be 15 years old. (The first 50 will be 13 and 14, the next 30 will be 15). The mode, if you recall, is the number that appears the most often—the 16-year-old-kids in this case—so the mode is 16. You don't need to list them out. The sum of 15 and 16 is 31, or **C**, the correct answer.

52 F Here's how to crack it: Domain goes in and range comes out. So you should plug each domain value into the function to determine what values the function spits out. **J** can be eliminated, because a function will have only one value for each domain range—and **J** has infinitely many values. When you plug in 5, the function spits out 19, which eliminates **H**(our correct answer must have 19). When we plug in 9, the function spits out 15.67—so we know **F** must be the correct answer:

$$\frac{5^2+13}{5-3} = \frac{38}{2} = 19$$

$$\frac{9^2+13}{9-3} = \frac{94}{6} = 15.67$$

53 D Here's how to crack it: Plug and chug!

$$(x+y)\ (x-y) \text{ is equal to}$$
$$(7+-3)(7--3) =$$
$$(4)(10) =$$
$$40$$

54 J Here's how to crack it: Plug the numbers into the formula for indirect variation,

$$y = \frac{k}{x}.$$

$$y = \frac{k}{x}$$

$$12 = \frac{k}{4}$$

$$k = 48$$

So, having established our constant as 48, we can solve for x when y is 6:

$$6 = \frac{48}{x}$$

$$x = 8$$

55 B Here's how to crack it: Plug into the formula, yet again:

$$F = \frac{\dfrac{(1000)}{.2} \bullet 5}{2} = \frac{5000 \bullet 5}{2} = 12{,}500$$

56 H Here's how to crack it: To solve for the x-intercepts, set the equation to 0 and then factor:

$$(x+13)(x-13) = 0$$
$$x = 13, x = -13$$

This means that our x-intercepts must be at 13 and -13, or **H**.

57 A Here's how to crack it: For the x-intercepts, set the equation to zero and solve:

$$x^2 + 5x - 14 = 0$$
$$(x+7)(x-2) = 0$$
$$x = -7, 2$$

To solve for the y-intercept, we plug in 0 for x, giving us -14.

Only **A** has the correct intercepts.

58 H Here's how to crack it: This question is tricky. Remember that the equation of a line must always be equal to a *SINGLE y*, which means we'll need to factor this equation to equal y before looking for it's graph.

$$2y - 4x = -6$$
$$2y = 4x - 6$$
$$\frac{2y}{2} = \frac{2(2x-3)}{2}$$
$$y = 2x - 3$$

From this point, it's fairly elementary. Only two lines have a y-intercept of -3, and only one has a positive slope, so the answer must be **C**.

59 C Here's how to crack it: Plug and chug!

$$3x^2 - 5xy + y^2$$
$$3(3)^2 - 5(3)(-4) + (-4)^2$$
$$27 + 60 + 16$$
$$103$$

60 J Here's how to crack it: 3 is your input, and −1 should be your output. Only **J** hits the spot.

$$x^2 - 10$$
$$3^2 - 10 = 9 - 10 = -1$$

Kevin Higginbotham currently teaches for the Nanjing University in Nanjing, China. He has also taught for The Princeton Review in Thailand. He is an avid scuba diver.

Completely darken bubbles with a No. 2 pencil. If you make a mistake, be sure to erase mark completely. Erase all stray marks.

1. YOUR NAME:
(Print)

Last | First | M.I.

SIGNATURE: _____ DATE: ___/___/___

HOME ADDRESS: _____
(Print)

Number

City | State | Zip Code

PHONE NO.: _____
(Print)

IMPORTANT: Please fill in these boxes exactly as shown on the back cover of your test book.

2. TEST FORM

3. TEST CODE

4. REGISTRATION NUMBER

5. YOUR NAME

First 4 letters of last name				FIRST INIT	MID INIT

(A)(A)(A)(A)(A)(A)
(B)(B)(B)(B)(B)(B)
(C)(C)(C)(C)(C)(C)
(D)(D)(D)(D)(D)(D)
(E)(E)(E)(E)(E)(E)
(F)(F)(F)(F)(F)(F)
(G)(G)(G)(G)(G)(G)
(H)(H)(H)(H)(H)(H)
(I)(I)(I)(I)(I)(I)
(J)(J)(J)(J)(J)(J)
(K)(K)(K)(K)(K)(K)
(L)(L)(L)(L)(L)(L)
(M)(M)(M)(M)(M)(M)
(N)(N)(N)(N)(N)(N)
(O)(O)(O)(O)(O)(O)
(P)(P)(P)(P)(P)(P)
(Q)(Q)(Q)(Q)(Q)(Q)
(R)(R)(R)(R)(R)(R)
(S)(S)(S)(S)(S)(S)
(T)(T)(T)(T)(T)(T)
(U)(U)(U)(U)(U)(U)
(V)(V)(V)(V)(V)(V)
(W)(W)(W)(W)(W)(W)
(X)(X)(X)(X)(X)(X)
(Y)(Y)(Y)(Y)(Y)(Y)
(Z)(Z)(Z)(Z)(Z)(Z)

6. DATE OF BIRTH

Month	Day	Year
JAN		
FEB		
MAR	(0)(0)	(0)(0)
APR	(1)(1)	(1)(1)
MAY	(2)(2)	(2)(2)
JUN	(3)(3)	(3)(3)
JUL	(4)	(4)(4)
AUG	(5)	(5)(5)
SEP	(7)	(7)(7)
OCT	(8)	(8)(8)
NOV	(9)	(9)(9)
DEC		

Test code / registration columns:
(0)(A)(0)(0)(0)(0)(0)(0)(0)(0)(0)
(1)(B)(1)(1)(1)(1)(1)(1)(1)(1)(1)
(2)(C)(2)(2)(2)(2)(2)(2)(2)(2)(2)
(3)(D)(3)(3)(3)(3)(3)(3)(3)(3)(3)
(4)(E)(4)(4)(4)(4)(4)(4)(4)(4)(4)
(5)(F)(5)(5)(5)(5)(5)(5)(5)(5)(5)
(7)(G)(7)(7)(7)(7)(7)(7)(7)(7)(7)
(8)(8)(8)(8)(8)(8)(8)(8)(8)(8)
(9)(9)(9)(9)(9)(9)(9)(9)(9)(9)

7. SEX
○ MALE
○ FEMALE

The Princeton Review
© 1996 Princeton Review L.L.C.
FORM NO. 00001-PR

Practice Test (1)

1. (A)(B)(C)(D)	21. (A)(B)(C)(D)	41. (A)(B)(C)(D)	61. (A)(B)(C)(D)
2. (F)(G)(H)(J)	22. (F)(G)(H)(J)	42. (F)(G)(H)(J)	62. (F)(G)(H)(J)
3. (A)(B)(C)(D)	23. (A)(B)(C)(D)	43. (A)(B)(C)(D)	63. (A)(B)(C)(D)
4. (F)(G)(H)(J)	24. (F)(G)(H)(J)	44. (F)(G)(H)(J)	64. (F)(G)(H)(J)
5. (A)(B)(C)(D)	25. (A)(B)(C)(D)	45. (A)(B)(C)(D)	65. (A)(B)(C)(D)
6. (F)(G)(H)(J)	26. (F)(G)(H)(J)	46. (F)(G)(H)(J)	66. (F)(G)(H)(J)
7. (A)(B)(C)(D)	27. (A)(B)(C)(D)	47. (A)(B)(C)(D)	67. (A)(B)(C)(D)
8. (F)(G)(H)(J)	28. (F)(G)(H)(J)	48. (F)(G)(H)(J)	68. (F)(G)(H)(J)
9. (A)(B)(C)(D)	29. (A)(B)(C)(D)	49. (A)(B)(C)(D)	69. (A)(B)(C)(D)
10. (F)(G)(H)(J)	30. (F)(G)(H)(J)	50. (F)(G)(H)(J)	70. (F)(G)(H)(J)
11. (A)(B)(C)(D)	31. (A)(B)(C)(D)	51. (A)(B)(C)(D)	71. (A)(B)(C)(D)
12. (F)(G)(H)(J)	32. (F)(G)(H)(J)	52. (F)(G)(H)(J)	72. (F)(G)(H)(J)
13. (A)(B)(C)(D)	33. (A)(B)(C)(D)	53. (A)(B)(C)(D)	73. (A)(B)(C)(D)
14. (F)(G)(H)(J)	34. (F)(G)(H)(J)	54. (F)(G)(H)(J)	74. (F)(G)(H)(J)
15. (A)(B)(C)(D)	35. (A)(B)(C)(D)	55. (A)(B)(C)(D)	75. (A)(B)(C)(D)
16. (F)(G)(H)(J)	36. (F)(G)(H)(J)	56. (F)(G)(H)(J)	76. (F)(G)(H)(J)
17. (A)(B)(C)(D)	37. (A)(B)(C)(D)	57. (A)(B)(C)(D)	77. (A)(B)(C)(D)
18. (F)(G)(H)(J)	38. (F)(G)(H)(J)	58. (F)(G)(H)(J)	78. (F)(G)(H)(J)
19. (A)(B)(C)(D)	39. (A)(B)(C)(D)	59. (A)(B)(C)(D)	79. (A)(B)(C)(D)
20. (F)(G)(H)(J)	40. (F)(G)(H)(J)	60. (F)(G)(H)(J)	80. (F)(G)(H)(J)

Completely darken bubbles with a No. 2 pencil. If you make a mistake, be sure to erase mark completely. Erase all stray marks.

1. YOUR NAME: _____
(Print)   Last   First   M.I.

SIGNATURE: _____ **DATE:** ____ / ____ / ____

HOME ADDRESS: _____
(Print)   Number

_____
City   State   Zip Code

PHONE NO.: _____
(Print)

IMPORTANT: Please fill in these boxes exactly as shown on the back cover of your test book.

2. TEST FORM

3. TEST CODE   **4. REGISTRATION NUMBER**

5. YOUR NAME

First 4 letters of last name				FIRST INIT	MID INIT

A A A A A A
B B B B B B
C C C C C C
D D D D D D
E E E E E E
F F F F F F
G G G G G G
H H H H H H
I I I I I I
J J J J J J
K K K K K K
L L L L L L
M M M M M M
N N N N N N
O O O O O O
P P P P P P
Q Q Q Q Q Q
R R R R R R
S S S S S S
T T T T T T
U U U U U U
V V V V V V
W W W W W W
X X X X X X
Y Y Y Y Y Y
Z Z Z Z Z Z

6. DATE OF BIRTH

Month	Day	Year
JAN		
FEB		
MAR	0 0	0 0
APR	1 1	1 1
MAY	2 2	2 2
JUN	3 3	3 3
JUL	4	4 4
AUG	5	5 5
SEP		7 7
OCT		8 8
NOV		9 9
DEC		

Test Code bubbles: 0 A, 1 B, 2 C, 3 D, 4 E, 5 F, 7 G, 8, 9 and numeric columns 0–9

7. SEX
○ MALE
○ FEMALE

The Princeton Review
© 1996 Princeton Review L.L.C.
FORM NO. 00001-PR

Practice Test ②

1. A B C D
2. F G H J
3. A B C D
4. F G H J
5. A B C D
6. F G H J
7. A B C D
8. F G H J
9. A B C D
10. F G H J
11. A B C D
12. F G H J
13. A B C D
14. F G H J
15. A B C D
16. F G H J
17. A B C D
18. F G H J
19. A B C D
20. F G H J

21. A B C D
22. F G H J
23. A B C D
24. F G H J
25. A B C D
26. F G H J
27. A B C D
28. F G H J
29. A B C D
30. F G H J
31. A B C D
32. F G H J
33. A B C D
34. F G H J
35. A B C D
36. F G H J
37. A B C D
38. F G H J
39. A B C D
40. F G H J

41. A B C D
42. F G H J
43. A B C D
44. F G H J
45. A B C D
46. F G H J
47. A B C D
48. F G H J
49. A B C D
50. F G H J
51. A B C D
52. F G H J
53. A B C D
54. F G H J
55. A B C D
56. F G H J
57. A B C D
58. F G H J
59. A B C D
60. F G H J

61. A B C D
62. F G H J
63. A B C D
64. F G H J
65. A B C D
66. F G H J
67. A B C D
68. F G H J
69. A B C D
70. F G H J
71. A B C D
72. F G H J
73. A B C D
74. F G H J
75. A B C D
76. F G H J
77. A B C D
78. F G H J
79. A B C D
80. F G H J

Practice Test Scoring Guide

Practice Test 1

Total 60 questions   ___/60 correct
– 10 Field-test items
(3, 11, 15, 21, 27, 30, 34, 45, 51, 58)   ___/10 correct

Total 50 questions   ___/50 correct

0–26 = failing
27–44 = passing
45–50 = advanced

Practice Test 2

Total 60 questions   ___/60 correct
– 10 Field-test items
(4, 12, 15, 23, 26, 31, 33, 43, 50, 56)   ___/10 correct

Total 50 questions   ___/50 correct

0–26 = failing
27–44 = passing
45–50 = advanced

Find the Right School

BEST 331 COLLEGES
2001 EDITION
The Smart Buyer's Guide to College
0-375-75633-7 • $20.00

THE COMPLETE BOOK OF COLLEGES
2001 EDITION
0-375-76152-7 • $26.95

THE GUIDE TO PERFORMING ARTS
PROGRAMS
Profiles of Over 600 Colleges, High
Schools and Summer Programs
0-375-75095-9 • $24.95

POCKET GUIDE TO COLLEGES
2001 EDITION
0-375-75631-0 • $9.95

AFRICAN AMERICAN STUDENT'S
GUIDE TO COLLEGE
Making the Most of College:
Getting In, Staying In, and
Graduating
0-679-77878-0 • $17.95

Get in

CRACKING THE SAT & PSAT
2001 EDITION
0-375-75621-3 • $18.00

CRACKING THE SAT & PSAT
WITH SAMPLE TESTS ON CD-ROM
2001 EDITION
0-375-75622-1 • $29.95

SAT MATH WORKOUT
2ND EDITION
0-375-76177-7 • $14.95

SAT VERBAL WORKOUT
2ND EDITION
0-375-76176-4 • $14.95

CRACKING THE ACT WITH
SAMPLE TESTS ON CD-ROM
2001 EDITION
0-375-76180-2 • $29.95

CRACKING THE ACT
2001 EDITION
0-375-76179-9 • $18.00

CRASH COURSE FOR THE ACT
10 Easy Steps to Higher Score
0-375-75376-5 • $9.95

CRASH COURSE FOR THE SAT
10 Easy Steps to Higher Score
0-375-75324-9 • $9.95

Get Help Paying for it

DOLLARS & SENSE FOR COLLEGE STUDENTS
How Not to Run Out of Money by Midterms
0-375-75206-4 • $10.95

PAYING FOR COLLEGE WITHOUT GOING BROKE
2001 EDITION
Insider Strategies to Maximize Financial Aid
and Minimize College Costs
0-375-76156-X • $18.00

THE SCHOLARSHIP ADVISOR
2001 EDITION
0-375-76160-8 • $25.00

Make the Grade with Study Guides for the AP and SAT II Exams

AP Exams

CRACKING THE AP BIOLOGY 2000-2001 EDITION
0-375-75495-4 • $17.00

CRACKING THE AP CALCULUS AB & BC 2000-2001 EDITION
0-375-75499-7 • $18.00

CRACKING THE AP CHEMISTRY 2000-2001 EDITION
0-375-75497-0 • $17.00

CRACKING THE AP ECONOMICS (MACRO & MICRO) 2000-2001 EDITION
0-375-75507-1 • $17.00

CRACKING THE AP ENGLISH LITERATURE 2000-2001 EDITION
0-375-75493-8 • $17.00

CRACKING THE AP EUROPEAN HISTORY 2000-2001 EDITION
0-375-75498-9 • $17.00

CRACKING THE AP PHYSICS 2000-2001 EDITION
0-375-75492-X • $19.00

CRACKING THE AP PSYCHOLOGY 2000-2001 EDITION
0-375-75480-6 • $17.00

CRACKING THE AP SPANISH 2000-2001 EDITION
0-375-75481-4 • $17.00

CRACKING THE AP U.S. GOVERNMENT AND POLITICS 2000-2001 EDITION
0-375-75496-2 • $17.00

CRACKING THE AP U.S. HISTORY 2000-2001 EDITION
0-375-75494-6 • $17.00

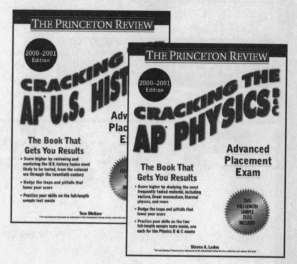

SAT II Exams

CRACKING THE SAT II: BIOLOGY 2001-2002 EDITION
0-375-76181-0 • $17.00

CRACKING THE SAT II: CHEMISTRY 2001-2002 EDITION
0-375-76182-9 • $17.00

CRACKING THE SAT II: FRENCH 2001-2002 EDITION
0-375-76184-5 • $17.00

CRACKING THE SAT II: LITERATURE & WRITING 2001-2002 EDITION
0-375-76183-7 • $17.00

CRACKING THE SAT II: MATH 2001-2002 EDITION
0-375-76186-1 • $18.00

CRACKING THE SAT II: PHYSICS 2001-2002 EDITION
0-375-76187-X • $17.00

CRACKING THE SAT II: SPANISH 2001-2002 EDITION
0-375-76188-8 • $17.00

CRACKING THE SAT II: U.S. & WORLD HISTORY 2001-2002 EDITION
0-375-76185-3 • $17.00

Expert Advice

www.review.com

Talk About It

www.review.com

Pop Surveys

Paying for it

www.review.com

The Princeton Review

www.review.com

Getting in

Word du Jour

Find-O-Rama School & Career Search

www.review.com

Finding it

Best Schools